Universe of Worlds

Also by Robert J. Grant

Love and Roses from David

Are We Listening to the Angels?

The Place We Call Home

Universe of Worlds

Exploring the Frontiers of the Afterlife

by Robert J. Grant

ARE
PRESS

**ASSOCIATION FOR
RESEARCH AND
ENLIGHTENMENT**

A.R.E. Press • Virginia Beach • Virginia

3rd Printing, November 2006

Printed in the U.S.A.

A.R.E. Press
215 67th Street
Virginia Beach, VA 23451-2061

Grateful acknowledgment is made to the following publisher for permission to reprint from their publication:

The Boy Who Saw True, by S.L. 1953. The C.W. Daniel Company Limited, 1 Church Path, Saffron Walden, Essex, England, CB10 1J. All rights reserved.

Library of Congress Cataloguing-in-Publication Data
Grant, Robert J.
    Universe of worlds : exploring the frontiers of the afterlife / by Robert J. Grant.
        p.   cm.
Includes bibliographical references. (p.   ).
    ISBN 0-87604-446-1 (trade pbk.)
    1. Spiritualism. 2. Future life–Miscellanea.   3. Death–Miscellanea. I. Title.
BF1261.2.G73 2005
133.9–dc21

2003000067

Cover design by Richard Boyle

For Scott Sparrow
*Who helped me find the Light
at the end of the tunnel*

Contents

For, the earth is only an atom in the universe of worlds.

Edgar Cayce reading 5749-3

Acknowledgments

I am deeply grateful for the inspiration and friendship of two very important mentors in my life: George G. Ritchie, M.D., and Raymond A. Moody, M.D. They have encouraged me to continue writing and speaking, and it was a joy for me to share the speaker's platform with them this last year.

I owe so much to my "literary mentor" and dear friend, Joseph P. Dunn, Jr., who departed this earthly life on September 11, 2001. Back in 1992, he took me under his wing, and I wrote my first book under his editorship. Even after forty-plus years in the publishing "arena" (and I use the term literally), he was always kind-hearted and compassionate to his writers, and his criticism was always constructive and helpful. I don't know where I would be today if I hadn't met Joe Dunn. He was and continues to be a light in my literary life.

Joe passed the editorial torch to Brenda English, a gifted writer and stellar editor. She is another rare bird in the literary field who has not lost any of the virtues I mentioned above. Writers are a neurotic lot. Impatience and harsh criticism from an editor can cut like a razor-sharp stiletto and bring a writer's creativity to a screeching halt. Brenda and Joe, together, edited my last book, *The Place We Call Home*, and I never screeched or halted, nor were there any knives waiting in the wings. I owe a great deal to Brenda English for her patience when I was going through a severe period of writer's block while writing *Universe of Worlds*. Joe could not have passed that editorial torch to a more professional, insightful, wise editor and writer when he passed it to Brenda. This book would not be in your hands were it not for her constant encouragement and reassurance that I could do it. God bless you, my friend.

I'm extremely grateful to Jean Harrington, who, with her late husband, Victor Harrington, amassed one of the most amazing private metaphysical libraries I have ever seen. Jean welcomed me into her home and invited me to conduct research for as long as I needed. Thank you, Jean; your home is literally like a "Hall of Records!"

Edgar Cayce said, "We often entertain angels unaware." Nikki Lockney is a human being, but she is also an angel. She came into my life like a heaven-sent light being and said, "Hi! I'd like to donate to you my mother's library of Edgar Cayce books. She was a member since the late 1940s and had tons of the old A.R.E. booklets. I think you're supposed to have them." I was stunned—happily so. I've been a collector of rare and out-of-print books for many years. "I was intuitively directed to give them to someone who would love them and treasure them as much as my mother did," Nikki said. What an honor! So many books go out of print in the blink of an eye these days, and I was delighted to receive this rare gift. Those rare Cayce books were an invaluable resource in writing *Universe of Worlds*. I also appreciated her friendship and encouragement during the writing of this book.

Last, but not least, I must thank the loving friends and family who were a source of material, emotional, and spiritual assistance during the writing of this book: My parents, George and Mary Lou Grant, and my friends and spiritual family, Lois Bennett, Michele A. Livingston, Bert and Mercedes Martinez, Levan Burgin, Ruth Easley Smith, GeorgeAn Barden, LaNette Kardokus, Claudeen Cowell, Michael Francis, Clinton Wallace, Kevin Todeschi, Bruce and Martie Shelton, Susan Thomas, Raymond Moody, M.D., George G. Ritchie, M.D., Jan Sloan, and last but *certainly* not least, my beloved friend, Helen Ruth Schroeder.

Preface
Experiences from Beyond the Veil

$\mathcal{S}$ometimes so-called *paranormal* or *supernatural* experiences happen to us under the most *normal* of circumstances in a very natural environment. That was my experience when my paternal grandmother, or "Grandma Hazel" Grant, came into the restaurant outside Camp Hill, Pennsylvania, where I was having dinner with my friend, Michele A. Livingston, a visionary artist, author[1], and gifted clairvoyant.

By the way, my Grandma Hazel Grant had been dead for twenty years when she popped into the restaurant. I didn't see her, but my friend Michele did. You see, Michele has the gift of being able to see through the "veil" that separates the material from the spiritual world and communicates with people on the other side, in much the same way as more well-known personalities such as John Edward, James Van Praagh, and Sylvia Browne. Michele and I together conducted seminars entitled "Beyond the Veil—Exploring the Eternal Nature of the Soul" in Harrisburg, Pennsylvania, in 1998 and 1999.

When my grandmother "came in," Michele looked puzzled for a moment and then said, "Someone from your family is here, Rob. She's got gray hair, glasses, and a very pronounced mole on her cheek near her nose. And she calls you 'Robbie.'"

From being around Michele, I had learned the truth of something that Hugh Lynn Cayce said about his late father, Edgar Cayce, who possessed psychic abilities that included the ability to see the so-called "dead" just as easily as he could see people in the physical world. "You never could tell," Hugh Lynn said, "what deceased person was going to show up and say something, or some paranormal event was going to happen right in the middle of an ordinary day." For me, this experience with my grandmother was an extraordinary event. Being as close as I am to Michele, such experiences with after-death communications had become a very "normal" part of our time together, but this was the first time a member of my own family had come through.

As Michele sat in silence, listening to my Grandma Hazel, a flash of happy childhood memories came back to me of being with Grandma. I remembered her playing with me and my older brothers, John and Jim, as if she were still a child herself. We had had a "Tarzan rope" swing tied to a huge oak tree in the backyard of our home in Indiana. We would stand on the sloping hillside beside the tree and swing way out, holding on to knotted sections of the rope with our hands and our feet. I always felt as if I were flying when I'd swing on the Tarzan rope. One day, Grandma came to watch us boys swing on the rope.

"Boy, that looks like fun," she said. "Hand it to me." My older brothers stood stock still for a moment. They didn't know what to do. "I said, hand me that rope, John." He shyly handed her the rope, disbelieving she would actually take the leap, but she grabbed onto the knot, wrapped her feet around the rope, and there she went! "Wheeeee!" Grandma said, as she swung out in an arc with the agility of a teenager and then swung back to the top of the hill just like a pro (If you missed your footing, you'd be left hanging at the bottom of the hill, a few feet off the ground). "Boy, that was great!"

I can remember seeing her gray-and-white house dress flapping in the wind. I remember seeing my brother John standing there with his mouth hanging open and his eyes bulging. It scared him to no end. I'm sure he thought she was going to crash into the tree or fall off and get hurt. I was six or seven and didn't know about fear. I just thought it so cool that Grandma did it. "Wow! Look at Grandma!" It endeared her to me no end.

As this memory flashed through my mind, I was filled with happy nostalgia. But then, uncomfortable memories came to mind just as swiftly. My grandmother was in a nursing home the last ten years of her life. I should say her *body* was in a nursing home during those years. There was nothing recognizable about Grandma in the final years of her life. She had senile dementia, as it was called back in the 1970s. No one knew much about Alzheimer's back then, so I don't know if that's what happened to her or not. I just remember that one day her mind was there and then it wasn't—and she had to be put into a nursing home. Anyway, the guilt came because I didn't go see Grandma during her years in the nursing home. I remember my cousin, Ann, returning from a visit to see her and saying, "Rob, you don't want to go. I don't know what that . . . that thing is in the nursing home, but it's not Grandma. It's her body, but that's all. She doesn't even look like herself. I wish I hadn't gone. You don't want to see her." Ann told me this in a state of utter shock and fear, as if she had seen something from a horror movie. Other members of the family said the same thing about Grandma.

I didn't go see her at all during those ten years. When she died, I was in the navy and couldn't get away to go to the funeral. Naturally, I felt guilty and remorseful.

Now, in the restaurant, I sat in a startled silence for a few moments after Michele accurately described my Grandma Hazel Grant. The emotions that ran through me were paradoxical; I felt the exhilaration and love for my grandmother that I'd felt as young boy, and I also felt regretful and guilt-ridden for not being with her, not even *seeing* her during her final years. I wondered what message she had come from the other side to give me.

Michele sat at the table, smiling, listening to my grandmother. After a few moments, she said, "Okay, this is what I'm picking up from her. She says, 'Tell Robbie not to feel badly about not seeing me in the nursing home. *I didn't spend a day there.*' And she says to be sure and tell the rest of your family this message."

I was, needless to say, amazed. Michele had no knowledge of my grandmother. We hadn't had much opportunity to talk about our families. This message surprised and relieved me. Many believe that, in certain instances, the soul can depart the body minutes, hours, days, weeks, even years before the physical body actually dies. I had come across this concept in *The Boy Who Saw True:*[2]

The idea of a body without a soul is, to an occultist, not as absurd as it may sound on the surface. Leaving aside the materialistic view that . . . a soul inhabits a body and vacates it at the moment of death. And yet, in the case of a certain number of aged people this is not always correct; for the soul has been known to leave the body some years prior to its final dissolution. When this occurs we have what is called 'second childhood'; a state which indicates that the soul has been left to the so-termed *body elemental* . . .

The body has a consciousness all its own, and that consciousness has the mentality of a child. My grandmother was infantile by the time the connection between body and soul was completely broken and she physically died. But that connection with the body doesn't hinder the soul from moving on and going about its work. It may "pop back in" from time to time, and, when that occurs, the person who has been in a near-comatose state or has been speaking gibberish will suddenly speak clearly, coherently, and will be fully lucid. They will recognize family members they haven't recognized for some time. Then, as quickly as they come back, they're gone again. The description of this state—in and out of consciousness—is accurate, but the truth of it at a deeper level is that *it is the soul going in and out of the body.*

It has been said that all souls leave the body during sleep and are doing work in the astral realms or in other worlds—being helpers and guides to other souls. Even though the body is at rest, the soul is free from the limitations of the physical world. This is also true in cases of advanced Alzheimer's or when the body is in a coma or being "child-like" or infantile. Why does this happen? I can draw only on my own experience to answer that question, and this was the very question I asked my grandmother through Michele.

"She seems to be fading from me, Rob," Michele had said, "Do you have anything you want to ask her?"

"Grandma, why did your body live so long without you being there?"

After a moment, Michele laughed and said, "Your grandmother says,

'I provided those nurses a nice living!'"

I laughed out loud. What a very practical, down-to-earth answer! Her soul had gone on, but the nurses were employed to take care of Grandma's body—which they did. I thought, "Boy, that sure sounds like something Grandma would do."

Through Michele, Grandma then said, "Tell Robbie I love him." With that, she was gone. What a tremendous weight was lifted from me. Michele and other seers, including Edgar Cayce, have said that feelings of guilt, remorse, or regret over things left unsaid or undone by those on earth are felt by those we love on the other side. In many instances, our guilt and remorse can hold the departed soul back from completely moving on—especially if those feelings are deeply held for a long time after a loved one's death. Many times, Edgar Cayce said to pray for the deceased, but not to condemn the circumstances of the passing or grieve for the departed. He said the soul has merely passed through "God's other door" (the term he used for death) and entered another world, a world of greater understanding and greater life.

Our loved ones who have passed on are aware of all the love we have for them, and they also feel any guilt or remorse we have. So, I wondered, "What kind of effect have I had on my Grandma Hazel with feeling guilty over not seeing her?" Because Grandma came back to give me her message through Michele, obviously she was picking up a great deal of these feelings from myself and other members of my family. That, I believe, is why she said to give the message to the rest of my family as well.

I have a very open-minded family who, because of our involvement with the Cayce work for more than twenty years, are very receptive and open to my "tales from the Beyond." I also believe that this experience has had a healing impact on my whole family. My aunt Myra (my grandmother's youngest daughter) told me that the last time she saw Grandma, Grandma uttered some words that devastated my aunt. At first, Grandma was sitting there in the nursing home in a vegetative state; then suddenly, it was as if she "stepped back in" momentarily. The life came back into her eyes, and Myra recognized the change immediately. But the only thing Grandma said to her was, "Why don't you just leave?"

Of course, this upset Myra to no end. During Grandma's life, she was not the most tactful person with adults, and, while she was a fun, loving, playful grandmother, she was rather harsh with her own children—particularly my aunt Myra. They had a rocky relationship for the better part of their lives together, and my Grandmother was the cause of a lot of upheaval and pain in Myra's life. Grandma's final words to Myra were typical of some of the harsh things she might have said to her, but, after I received the message from Grandma through Michele, I understood what Grandma was telling Myra in a more constructive light. What she was really saying to Myra was, "Why don't you just leave? There's nobody here, Myra. You're talking to the body. Go on, get out of here, and get on with your life. I have." Perhaps Grandma could only get those few words out to my aunt Myra because Grandma had been "out" for so long. When I explained my new understanding to Myra, I believe she, too, came to a new understanding of her mother's words, and I hope the experience enabled some healing to happen for her. Grandma wasn't insulting Myra; she was simply telling her, "The lights are on but nobody's home."

This experience prompted me to delve into Cayce's psychic "readings" on the death transition a bit deeper, and I looked up some of the readings for people who were close to death. Sure enough, I found readings in which Cayce said that, while the "entity" (a word he often used for the soul) was present, it was just waiting for the final separation from the body or that the soul had already left the body and the body needed nothing except care until the final separation.

The mysteries of death and where the soul goes after death are becoming clearer and clearer. Sometimes, however, it seems that the more we find out about the hereafter, the more new questions come up. In this book, which picks up the transiting soul about where *The Place We Call Home* left it, I wanted to delve more deeply into the realms of the afterlife, to help the reader become more familiar with the "final journey." Hugh Lynn Cayce told me, "Study and meditate to find the Light here and now . . . in meditation and in your dreams . . . if you find it here, you can be sure you'll go directly to the Light after death . . . but prepare now for that journey . . . for we each are building where we will go after death, day by day."

It is with this advice in mind that I wrote *Universe of Worlds*, to explore the deeper implications of the near–death experience as well as facets of the unseen worlds, their sacred inhabitants, and how they can and do direct us—in both our material lives and the life hereafter.

I've always been intrigued by the spiritual entities that make up what Edgar Cayce called "the unseen forces," and I hope that readers will come away from this book with a deeper understanding of how close every human being is to the myriad of spiritual worlds unseen and to helpful, benevolent beings who have been assigned to assist humanity in its spiritual awakening. I am more reassured than ever that we do not travel the earthly road alone—even though, at times, the road is hard, long, challenging, and painful. I believe there is a place where we can access the realms of spirit and hear the voice of the Creator (who speaks through the angels, archangels, and the elders of the Great White Brotherhood) say, "All is well . . . My peace I give you . . . my strength and courage to carry on, I give unto you . . . "

In this time of global upheaval, where fear and darkness have touched virtually everyone—especially since the terrorist attack on the World Trade Center on September 11, 2001—it is clear more than ever that the answers and the solace we seek are not in the material world, but in "the secret place of the Most High" within the heart of every human being. There, we can find the peace the passes understanding and then share that peace and understanding to help others who are faltering and fearful in the darkness. I hope the variety of subjects explored in *Universe of Worlds* will help readers find calm in the midst of the storm and understand the truth of what Edgar Cayce said, that no soul enters the earthly experience alone, and no soul departs this realm alone. Further, it is my hope that readers will realize the spiritual worlds so interpenetrate our physical world that they are not far from us at all. As Edgar Cayce said, " . . . the earth is only an atom in the universe of worlds."

Robert J. Grant,
Virginia Beach, Va.
January 2003

Introduction

. . . life itself is continuous, and the conditions of the whole of existence remain precisely as before. Circumstances have changed for the individual, but only in the sense that he is now aware of a different group of facts. The change of surroundings is a subjective one. The facts were of course there, all the time, as the stars are there in the daytime; but they were out of our ken. Now these come into our ken, and others fade into memory . . .

Sir Oliver Lodge
Raymond—Or Life and Death

*A*fter the publication of my third book, *The Place We Call Home: Explorations of the Soul's Existence After Death*, I had the opportunity to travel, speak at seminars and workshops about the afterlife, and meet hundreds of people from all walks of life. Many of these people had extraordinary stories to tell. Some had had near–death experiences. Scores of others freely admitted at my presentations that they knew they had experienced an after–death encounter with a loved one, either during a dream or meditation or actually seeing a visual apparition while awake. I was awed by how many people had read my book and wrote to me to tell their stories and share their experiences with the other side. For those who were attending their first spiritually based seminar, the stories that people shared publicly changed lives. Most people didn't come to hear me speak out of simple curiosity; they came because they were bereaved: Parents who had children who'd passed on before them (the most difficult experience in any lifetime), and widows, widowers, and best friends who felt they had to say good-bye too soon to the people they loved and cherished.

It isn't a belief of mine that life continues after the physical body dies; I *know* that it does. I spent many years working at the Association for Research and Enlightenment in Virginia Beach, Va., the organization founded in 1931 by Edgar Cayce, the preeminent American mystic and seer. The thousands of hours I spent working directly with Cayce's psychic "readings" (which were carefully transcribed when they were given) put me in a unique position to share with others my insights from the Cayce readings about the continuity of life both before and after death. Cayce communicated with the other side as easily as we see one another in this physical realm. He was able, psychically, to witness his own mother's transition from physical life to spiritual life. She didn't make the transition alone, but was in the company of relatives and friends who had passed on before her.

When loved ones make the journey to the afterlife before us and we must say our good-byes too soon in this world, it is only a temporary parting. There will be a reunion. Physical death cannot destroy the bonds of love we have built with one another. Both our consciousness and our loving bonds survive the transition of death and the journey to a dimension of Spirit. The essence of that Spirit is eternal, the substance of our souls. Physics says matter can neither be created nor destroyed, it can only change form. So it is with our true consciousness—our souls. At death, we journey to the next stage of life. We step through what Edgar Cayce called "God's other door" and leave the body behind.

In his psychic readings, Cayce also compared death to the change of seasons. The seasons come, go, and come again, in an "eternal return." So it is with our souls. We might say that the earthly life is like the spring, and the afterlife is summer. In fact, this is how many have described the beautiful dimension they witnessed on the other side during near-death experiences—as *the Summerland.*

I wanted to explore this realm in detail in this book because it sounded, from the corresponding descriptions that have come through mediums and clairvoyants over many decades, to be like Heaven. The Summerland is not the ultimate Heaven, they explain, but a beautiful stopping-off point, a way station of sorts, where the soul goes to rest after death, to reflect on the lessons learned in the life on earth, and, most importantly, to pick up in its development where life in the physical world left off.

You will learn here that the earth is a "shadow" of that which exists in the spiritual dimensions. Every material thing, according to the Cayce readings, has its source in the spiritual dimensions. The earth is a third-dimension projection of fourth-dimensional reality. The material world is the materialization of the spiritual worlds. In this light, it's not really surprising that the majority of people who have had near-death experiences said that being out of their physical body was the most natural feeling they had ever felt.

The spiritual realms are home; the earth is a school. But what lessons are we learning in that school—and that we continue to study on the other side?

Regardless of outward appearances, every soul is on a road to becoming an unconditionally loving being. According to the Cayce readings, when our every response to every situation, to every person, every day, is from love, then we can become "co-creators with God." Such advanced development may seem far, far away as we look around us at the world today. But no act of love, kindness, or compassion is ever in vain. All helpful thoughts, deeds, and intentions toward our fellow human beings lift up not only the other person, but ourselves and the entire universe as well.

Just as important as the knowledge that we are learning about love is the knowledge that it is the *trying* that counts. It's easy to belittle ourselves and criticize our failings and our undoings, but in the afterlife, we will see that the important focus of our learning is on what we intended. In the physical world everything seems to be "end-result oriented." In the spiritual world, it is a dimension of cause. After death, we will be asked what was the cause of what we did on earth. What was the motivating force behind what we did? Was it love? Indifference? Hate? Forgiveness? The thoughts that go into our actions on earth are powerful forces; on the other side, they become the worlds we experience. Edgar Cayce said the places in which we find ourselves on the other side are as unique as each individual. Dying, like birth, is a universal experience. But while we might all be born into the earth the same way, the *environment* and family situation into which we are born are uniquely our own. It is the same with the afterlife, and it is our thoughts and intentions here on earth that determine what we will experience—at least initially—in the afterlife.

Many people have had glimpses of the many worlds that exist on the other side. But even though we can know that life continues after death, that doesn't necessarily alleviate the pain of witnessing the death of the body. Many times, however, there is a glimpse of something more. The experiences of the people about whom I've written here touched me to the depths of my soul. One experience in particular stands out in my heart and memory.

While speaking in Canada, I had the opportunity to meet with a man whose son had died very young. George Kennedy was at the bedside of his son when he was dying. In the middle of the most painful experience George had ever had, watching his son die, he also had what he believes was a divine experience. While lying in his son's hospital bed and holding the boy, George experienced what Raymond Moody, M.D., calls a *"death coincident."* Someone who is with the dying at the time of death witnesses the spiritual side of dying in some form. Some have seen angels come into the room and remove the soul from the body. Others have seen the all-knowing, all-loving light so often spoken of in near-death experiences.

George's experience was transformative and healing and has stayed with him since his son passed in the early 1990s. With his eyes closed while holding his son, George felt himself rise above the bed, his son still in his arms, and then in his mind's "eye," he saw Jesus the Christ standing above him, arms outstretched. George looked in awe at this benevolent, all-loving spirit and understood what he was to do. Without hesitation, he physically placed his son in the arms of Jesus. As Jesus took his son, George found himself back on the bed, lying with his son and tears streaming down his face. Then he realized that his son had passed on simultaneously with George's vivid spiritual experience. George Kennedy is a down-to-earth man who believes he knows the difference between dreams and real-life experiences. This, he said, was the most real experience he has ever felt. He is comforted and knows that his son was taken care of as he died and is taken care of still.

People have asked me if such experiences are "thought forms" that are created by the individual's mind to make the suffering less difficult. I don't believe that what George saw was an illusion of wishful thinking. I believe that Jesus, the Master Soul, was there to take care of his son. Edgar Cayce said that God is so cognizant of each soul that He loves each of us without condition and sends angels and the Master to help us cross that bridge from this world to the next. Edgar Cayce said that our souls do not enter the unseen world alone.

My desire to write another book on dying and the afterlife was born from my conversations with the people I have met in the three years since *The Place We Call Home* was published. I soon realized there was much more to be said about the infinite dimensions of life after physical death. It would be impossible to chronicle all the details of the afterlife; there is no map, but there are guides. Our guides and our experiences after death seem to be the culmination of the love we have learned in our hearts for our fellow human beings. The love we cultivate, the compassion we show on earth, our simple acts of kindness all help build a gateway filled with divine Light. Edgar Cayce said Heaven is not a place that we go to, but that it is a place we grow to, on the arm of someone we have helped. Where we go from here on earth has everything to do with where we are now in heart and mind.

This concept really came home in powerful ways when I researched the source material for this book. There are beautiful experiences in this book. There are also some frightening aspects—the consequences of living a loveless life on earth. But *there is always redemption.* In the afterlife, we alone judge our lives on earth. God casts no soul from His presence; it is our own soul that can banish itself into realms of darkness and earthbound states. But just as we have opportunities every day to make a new start, so do souls on the other side. They must ask for help, however, from the higher realms, from the benevolent beings who help souls in the "lower" levels. But the soul, alone, must ask for that help; no one can do it for them. Even on earth, we've all probably had the experience of trying to help someone who hasn't asked for or who doesn't want our help; it doesn't work. But if we ask for that help, it is always given—both here and in the afterlife. We live in a universe of worlds—seen and unseen—and a universe of love and hope.

Death Hath No Sting

The mark of your ignorance is the depth of your belief in tragedy and injustice.
What the caterpillar calls the end of the world, the master calls a butterfly.

Richard Bach—*Illusions*

When Jan Manette[1] awoke at 8:30 a.m. on September 11, 2001, she was in a state of panic. She had slept right through the blaring clock radio alarm, and was a half-hour late for work. It wouldn't have been such a bad situation, but Jan was doing consulting work for the Pentagon, and this was only her second week on the job. Jan telephoned her office and told the receptionist she was running late.

After a quick shower, Jan dressed in a hurry, grabbed her briefcase and maneuvered through the heavy Washington, D.C., traffic.

"I've always prided myself on being punctual," Jan said. "And being late to anything is my biggest pet peeve; this [situation] was worse because it was only my second week on the job. On top of all that stress, I was just really perplexed; I went to bed the night before around 11:00 p.m. I *always* hear my alarm, and usually I'm awake before it goes off."

Getting to the Pentagon was difficult. Traffic was heavy, which only increased Jan's anxiety. When the Pentagon finally came into view, she felt her anxiety subside, but its easing would be short lived.

"After dealing with the D.C. traffic," Jan said, "I felt relieved when I finally saw the Pentagon, but I saw something hovering over the building and all of a sudden, I was afraid . . . It's hard to explain, but this feeling of dread came over me. I saw what looked like a huge, black, oval mass or cloudlike thing on top of the Pentagon. Above that was a white, floating mass like a puffy cloud. But my attention was drawn to the black, oval shape. I mean it was *black*—blacker than any color I've ever seen. I knew that it wasn't a cloud or smoke because of the shape— it was oval in shape, symmetrical—and the strangest thing about it was that it was perfectly still—unmoving. It was resting on top of part of the Pentagon and seemed to go up maybe ten or fifteen feet. I can't even describe how awful I felt just looking at it. I know it sounds crazy, but if I could describe that black thing in one word, it would be *evil*. Directly above this layer of black was a large, oval mass of white. It didn't touch the blackness. It seemed to hover above it the way a parachute looks when it's open in the air, or an umbrella. It was the most brilliant white I've ever seen. I can't describe exactly how it looked, but its shape, too, was totally symmetrical and seemed to hover over the dark thing. Have you ever seen the yin–yang symbol? It was kind of like that, except the white extended higher than the black. I saw these for only an instant. Looking back, it was like everything was in slow motion."

It's not uncommon for people who are involved in or witness a traumatic event to later report that time seemed to slow down; what happens in a matter of seconds imprints itself on the mind as if the event went on for hours. That was Jan's experience as she observed the strange black and white masses, and then witnessed the plane crashing into the Pentagon. What Jan saw before the plane crashed was, in her words, "the most powerful, unexplainable thing I've ever seen."

Jan said she realized that she had seen the souls of those killed at the Pentagon, departing the earthly realm, *before* the plane crash occurred.

"In terms of actual time, the complete experience couldn't have lasted more than a few seconds," Jan said. "I still can't make sense of that aspect of the whole experience. It was like I received a life-transforming understanding of what happens in cases of sudden, traumatic death, in the span of perhaps seconds." From the time Jan noticed the strange black and white masses above the Pentagon until the time the terrorist attack occurred was less than a minute. What she saw next was even more horrifying.

"I heard and then saw the plane heading straight for the Pentagon,"

Jan said, "and it was like seeing something totally incomprehensible. My mind just couldn't believe what I was seeing. Before the plane crashed, it was as if everything went into slow motion, literally. I can't explain it better than that; it was like watching a movie on my VCR and clicking the remote to watch a scene in slow motion. The plane was heading for the Pentagon and was still some distance from it. All at once, I saw these round, spherelike orbs of light rising up out of the plane. Dozens of them came out of the plane, and then it seemed as if hundreds of them rose out of the roof of the Pentagon. Everything was in slow motion except these round lights. They zoomed upward in a sort of spiral motion—all of them together—upward through that awful blackness and then they disappeared into the whiteness."

As Jan watched the light phenomena, she was filled with what she called, "the realization of an absolute truth" of what she was seeing. It is frustrating for her to try to describe how she received the message: It came to her instantaneously, the way the answer to a dilemma or problem may suddenly dawn in the mind.

"In the midst of this horrible thing happening," she said, "this instantaneous knowledge filled my entire being, and I was divinely reassured. I knew that those zooming spheres of light were the souls of the people who were going to die in the crash. I knew they were removed from their bodies before the actual crash into the Pentagon."

Jan talked with others who witnessed the terrorist attack at the Pentagon. No one that she spoke with saw the strange black and white forms above the roof; no one saw the orbs of lights. Nevertheless, Jan believes there was a spiritual reason for her having this experience.

"My spiritual life really began on that day, September 11," Jan said. "On the one hand, I felt relieved that I was saved; had I not overslept, I probably would be dead. But, on the other hand, I felt guilty—like 'Why me?' I've been in counseling since all this happened, and I've found that survivor's guilt is very common. I've suffered from periods of depression and post-traumatic stress from witnessing the plane crash. And yet in the midst of all the mixed emotions, I'm filled with a sense of serenity and relief from the vision I had. It has sustained me and given me peace when before I would cry over the loss of all those lives. God cannot stop the terrible things we humans do to one another, like the terrorist attacks on the Pentagon and the World Trade Center, but He *is* present at the darkest times of traumatic situations. I know He is taking care, 'behind the scenes', of the souls involved, no matter how bad it might appear."

Perhaps Jan survived and witnessed the vision that this story might be told. In the Creator's infinite care and love, perhaps He implanted a mystical understanding in Jan's heart and soul that, although we grieve for the sudden physical loss of friends and loved ones, there is safe passage for their souls—before the trauma, before the horror. Jan's vision did not make the horror go away, nor did it remove the grief of losing close friends, but it awakened in her an understanding that, to the soul, death does not exist. It is but a passage. Jan knew it was true. She had seen it with her own eyes.

Jasper Swain's seventeen–year–old son, Mike, was killed in a tragic car accident on the busy National Highway in South Africa, heading to Pietermaritzburg. Mike had been visiting his girlfriend's parents in Johannesburg to watch the auto races in Kejalami. Mike had completed his high school final exams, and he was looking forward to his first year of college at the University of Durban, in the fall.

An hour before the car accident, Mike was driving with his girlfriend, Moira, and another friend. Space was at a premium in the tiny subcompact car, and, after a brief rest stop in Harrisburg, Moira and the friend rode the rest of trip with Moira's parents, Bill and Maureen. Moira's eleven–year–old sister, Heather, worshipped Mike like a big brother and was happy to ride with him in the little car. Traffic was heavy as they pulled out onto the two–lane highway. Bill noticed a spiffy looking, late–model German car approaching them in the two–way traffic.

"Look," Bill said, "There's one of those new [German cars]." He glanced into his rearview mirror to admire the car as it passed, and, suddenly, the German car went airborne. The front of the car reared up, flipping the car end over end, and then it crashed to the ground in a shuddering heap.

Mike's little car was nowhere to be seen. Bill slammed on his brakes and managed to make a U-turn. When the dust and smoke cleared, Bill and Maureen couldn't believe what they saw. The German car and

Mike's car had collided head-on. The subcompact was on the side of the highway, mangled beyond belief. Only the rear tires were intact. Heather and Mike were killed on impact. The German car lay on its side. The driver had been thrown through the windshield and lay bleeding and motionless in the road. Bill and Maureen tried to free Heather and Mike from the wreckage, but it was useless. Crowds of people surrounded the scene of the accident. A young physician pushed his way through the crowd and examined Mike and Heather.

"I'm sorry," the doctor said to Bill and Maureen. A young couple traveling to Rhodesia offered to take Bill and Maureen to a nearby hotel. Bill refused to leave the scene until Mike's and Heather's bodies were freed from the wreckage. It took the wrecker crew more than an hour to pry the bodies from the tiny car. Bill and Maureen were taken to the hotel and a message was sent to Mike's parents, Jasper and Clarice Swain, in Pietermaritsburg.

Jasper, Clarice, and their youngest son, Kevin, drove in silence to the Colenzo Hotel. Jasper was filled with rage over the death of his son. He vowed vengeance upon whomever was responsible for Mike's death. Anger often serves as a shield to defend against emotions of loss, pain, and grief. Jasper clung to his rage and anger like a life raft to avoid feeling the pain. He fought back tears and tightened his grip on the steering wheel. Suddenly, a radiant presence of light was beside Jasper in the car. When he turned to look at Clarice, Jasper clearly saw a golden image of his son sitting next to him.

"Don't do anything stupid," Mike said, looking directly at his father. "Don't be a fool."

Jasper shook his head in disbelief. When he glanced again at the passenger seat, Mike was gone, but that moment of illumination dispelled Jasper's rage. He knew his son would not have approved of his vow of vengeance, nor was it generally in Jasper's nature to be vengeful. Jasper's rage was replaced by a sense of confusion and frustration, by wondering why things happened as they did. Jasper's sense of desolation and despair deepened when he realized that he would never really know why this tragedy had happened, why his son's life was cruelly cut short.

For those left behind, this is the most paralyzing aspect of dealing with sudden death: There is no answer to the burning question of "Why?" Pondering this unanswerable question only deepens the anger, despair, emptiness, and sense of loss.

Jasper Swain was wrong, however. He would find answers to the seemingly unanswerable questions and in a most unusual way.

An outpouring of support and sympathy, in the form of cards, letters, and flowers, flooded Jasper's office. Among the many messages waiting for Jasper, one stood out from the rest: A Mrs. Merrington had telephoned from Sezela on the South Coast with the following message: "As you once helped one in life, I will now help you in death."

Jasper put the message aside. Although he was open–minded and had studied many religions and spiritual philosophies, he didn't find comfort or solace in any of them—especially now that his son had died. Jasper tried to push the mysterious message out of his mind, but he was unable to do so. Something kept urging him, to the point of obsession, to "Go to Sezela. Go to Sezela. Go to Sezela."

Finally, Jasper could ignore the persistent message no longer. Although he had no idea where Sezela was, except that it was on the lower South Coast, Jasper got into his car and drove toward Durban. He stopped to ask for directions and discovered the Sezela was a sugar mill estate—and that was no more than a mile or so ahead. His inner guidance had sent him not only in the correct direction, but almost to the front door. Jasper drove up to the main gate and was directed to the office. There he met Mr. Merrington, who startled Jasper even more.

"You must be Jasper Swain," Mr. Merrington said, "Mike told my wife to expect you here this morning." Jasper felt as if he had wandered into some surreal play. He was completely at a loss for words as Mr. Merrington led him to a sitting room to meet his wife. Even more amazingly, Jasper recognized Mrs. Merrington. Though he hadn't remembered her name, some nine years earlier, he had conducted some pro bono legal work for her, at a time when she was at a low point and in desperate need. Her first husband had abandoned her, with two children to raise and no means of support. Jasper had assisted in the divorce proceedings and had seen to it that she was well taken care of. She subsequently had married Mr. Merrington, and it was obvious they were very close.

As Jasper sat across from Mrs. Merrington, he watched as she put her hands over her eyes and appeared to go into a trance. To his astonishment, she then began speaking in Mike's voice. Jasper's disbelief was quickly dispelled when Mike, speaking through Mrs. Merrington, called Jasper by the nickname "Chud." It was a name that only Mike had used— not even Clarice or Kevin knew of this name.

For the next hour, Mike—speaking through Mrs. Merrington—provided details of the fatal accident. He reassured Jasper that he was indeed alive and well. At the end of the hour, Mrs. Merrington came back to herself and said that she must rest. Jasper found himself in a state of complete joy and awe. He shook Nina Merrington's hand and quietly asked if he could bring his family to another sitting. Mrs. Merrington was happy to oblige.

Once he was home again, Jasper could barely contain himself as he announced to Clarice and Kevin that he had communicated with Mike. After assuring them he hadn't lost his mind, he implored them to come with him to the Merringtons' estate. The following afternoon, the Swains all sat in the Merringtons' sitting room. As before, Mrs. Merrington placed her hands over her eyes and entered into a trance state. The family looked at one another in amazement as Mike's voice spoke through Nina Merrington's vocal chords. Clarice and Kevin's doubts about Mike's presence were quickly dispelled—it was their beloved Mike, though the vocal chords were those of Mrs. Merrington.

When the family asked about the circumstances of the car accident, Mike said he would place Nina Merrington in the driver's seat so she could describe exactly how things had transpired.

"It is a terribly hot day," she said, "and I am driving along a very crowded road. There is a little girl beside me. Her name is Heather . . . Now I see a black car coming towards us. As it approaches us, I see this other car coming behind it. I can see this other car clearly, because it is in the middle of the road, trying to pass the black car . . . The sun is glaring on the windscreen of the black car and reflecting back into my eyes. I can see nothing but a bright silver radiance. All of a sudden, the radiance changes from silver to gold. I am being lifted up in the air, out through the top of the car. I grab little Heather's hand. She, too, is being lifted up out of the car.

"We have been lifted thirty feet above the [car]. And in one horrifying second, I see [it] and this large car collide head on . . . The large car is turning in mid-air . . . A storm of metallic dust is now glinting all over the road . . . "[2]

What made such an impact upon Jasper and his family was the fact that Mike had never seen the other vehicle until after the silver light had changed to gold. He and Heather had felt no sense of impact. They had suffered no pain, just a gentle ascent into the air.

"Heather and I are still holding hands," Mike continued. "We now descend beside the [car]. We see the two crumpled bodies lying in it . . . We both fully understand that we are, now, so far as mortals are concerned, dead. We are also both aware that a lot of people have begun to gather around us. They are dressed in glorious colors. We recognize familiar faces; the faces of friends who passed beyond the earth before us. We are still hand in hand; now, guided by the one who first lifted us into the air, the two of us sweep towards the skies."[3]

When Jasper wrote of listening to this account of Mike's passing, he said, "In heartfelt joy the three of us listened, transported by the fact that the passing had involved neither fear, shock, nor suffering."

Mike went on to discuss the place that now was his home. "There are not so much 'worlds' of existence, Dad, as planes of existence," he said. "Though we have the sun and the skies and acres of beautiful flowers here, we don't have rain, as you people know it. Nor is there any blight to destroy the beauty of the trees. They look exactly the same as they do on earth. With one big difference, however. Here, they are all perfect . . . "

Mike said his greatest joy there was the feeling of complete freedom, in an infinite world, to go wherever he wished, whenever he wished. He explained that, although others on this plane were at the same stage of development as him, he was still an individual, still himself, just as he had been on earth.

"This world is the right one for me at this stage of my development; but as my vibrations become more refined, I shall be able to visit the higher planes with ease," he said. "As we grow in spirit, we ascend to the next plane; the two processes worked hand-in-glove."[4]

As Mike described many things about his continuing life in the next world, his family was reassured beyond words that they had not "lost" their son, except in body. Mike let them know that, whenever the family thought of him with love, light, and fond memories, he experienced those things with them. Nor, he said, was his earthly life cut short; he had chosen to come to the earth for only a brief period of seventeen years. What appeared as an accident to the living was actually just a point of departure for the soul at the chosen time.

"If the circumstances of someone's passing look tragic," Mike said through Mrs. Merrington," I assure you Dad, it is only the appearance—to the soul, there's no experience of trauma or pain—only the awareness of moving into Light."

Jasper Swain's life changed in ways as a result of his subsequent friendship with Nina Merrington. He went on to have many communication sessions with his son, about the afterlife, and the most important thing Mike emphasized was learning to love while on earth. All that we can learn about love, forgiveness, kindness, and compassion will transport the soul, after death, to a glorious place of light beyond description, Mike said. The more we manifest light and love here on earth, the closer we gravitate to the Source of light and love, after death.

2

Edgar Cayce's Visions
Beyond the Veil

In earth, then, as has been seen, we are given—men, women—are given an opportunity—see what you do with it all! . . . the soul enters in, to make manifest its concept of . . . the first cause [God]! Being endowed with that spark . . . it enters in earth where all, in this sphere, are one! . . . a soul enters . . . taking on a form . . . to make manifest itself . . . it has flown out from its source to try its wings, to seek its own doing—or undoing; dependent upon that as has been builded, and the use it makes of that given it.

Edgar Cayce reading 311-2[1]

When Edgar Cayce entered into an unconscious trance state to give a reading, the scope of his psychic abilities was seemingly unlimited. He was able, during the majority of his readings, to answer any question posed to him on any subject. It wasn't uncommon for Cayce to answer the questions submitted by the seeker even before they were asked. His unconscious mind's ability to retrieve information startled even the waking Edgar Cayce. Upon awakening, he retained no memory of what transpired during the reading. Cayce sometimes remembered vivid dreams and spiritual visions during his readings, but he was completely unaware of the words he spoke while in trance.

Cayce's longtime secretary and stenographer, Gladys Davis, transcribed all the readings Cayce gave from 1923 until his death in 1945. "He gave over 14,000 readings during his lifetime," Gladys said more than once, "but he never heard one. He'd wake up from the reading and say, 'Did we get it?' or 'Did I say anything that will help them?' Mr. Cayce needed reassurance that the readings were helping people. His ability to give readings was like something apart from him since he couldn't remember what he said."

In the trance state, Edgar Cayce's unconscious mind was clairvoyant. *The Random House College Dictionary* defines clairvoyance as, "The alleged supernatural power of seeing objects or actions . . . beyond the range of natural vision." In *Webster's Collegiate Dictionary*, clairvoyance is defined simply as "second sight." Cayce's clairvoyant faculty enabled him to obtain accurate information for people, many of whom he had never met.

The range of Edgar Cayce's psychic ability was not hindered by distance, time, or space. Sometimes he made side comments in an undertone at the beginning of the reading, describing the activities happening around the person for whom he was giving the reading, even though that person might be thousands of miles away from Cayce. These asides sounded as if he were with the person instead of lying with closed eyes on the couch in his Virginia Beach home. Many of the comments Cayce made in such instances were verified and found to be accurate, as was the case with these three examples:

- "Yes, keep quiet," Cayce said in one reading, "they have an accident right in front of the house." This reading, 599-1, was given for a man hundreds of miles away from where Cayce was giving the reading.
- "That's a right pretty tree on the corner," Cayce said, in reading 1100-27. The woman for whom he gave the reading later wrote, "Yes, there is an unusually lovely tree at the corner of our apartment building."
- While giving reading 3904-1 for someone in New York City, Edgar Cayce, in Virginia Beach said, "Very unusual in some of these halls isn't it? What funny paintings!"

In addition to showing him places and events, Cayce's clairvoyant mind also had the ability to discern who needed a reading the most. On one occasion, Gertrude Cayce and Gladys Davis were late getting started on a series of follow-up or "check" health readings for a series of people. After Edgar Cayce entered the trance state, Gertrude Cayce read the name and address of the first person for whom Edgar was to give a reading. Instead of accepting the suggestion and locating the woman in New York City, Cayce said, "Better begin with [949]—he is going out!" Mr. [949]'s case had been put at the bottom of the list, but Gertrude accepted the unconscious advice and gave the Hollywood, California, address of Mr. [949]. From there, Cayce gave his physical check reading. When Mr. [949] received his reading, with the instructions to move it up to the first reading for that session, he wrote back that he, indeed, had been readying to leave his apartment at 8:30 p.m., Pacific Standard Time, which coincided with the time of the reading, 11:30 a.m., Eastern Standard Time.

Not only did Cayce say in trance that there was no real separation between the material world and the spirit world, but also he experienced this melding of the two in his waking hours. He was able to see emanating color patterns surrounding people—we call such patterns auras—and unless he "tuned out" what he saw in those patterns, he was able to pick up a great many things about the personalities of people around him. There were times, however, when the patterns he saw were so strong that he couldn't tune them out—and, no doubt, he wished that he could have. For instance, in his Sunday School class, he was able to "see" with his clairvoyant vision the souls of the young men who soon would be going off to fight in World War II and which of them would be killed in battle.

Seeing auras was just one conscious manifestation of his psychic ability that emphasized to Cayce the existence of souls and their survival after death. There were others as well. For instance, while teaching Sunday School one morning, he watched a group of people enter the church, sit down in the pews, and listen attentively to his Sunday School message. What was strange about this was that this group of people was from the spirit realms; all of them were deceased. No one except Cayce was aware of their presence. When unusual phenomena such as this happened, Cayce often sought the counsel of his own readings, such as the one that follows, that had much to say about the continuing development of the soul after death:

[Gertrude Cayce]: You will have before you the body and the soul-mind of Edgar Cayce, present in this room, and the experience or vision had by him on October 30th while teaching the Sunday School lesson at the First Presbyterian Church, Virginia Beach, Va., in which he saw a number of the Jewish faith apparently enter the church and listen at the discourse. You will please tell this body if this was a true vision, and just what, if anything, he is to do about it.

[Edgar Cayce]: Yes, we have the body, the enquiring mind and the soul-body Edgar Cayce, present in this room, and the experience, the vision had by the body while discoursing on the lesson.

As should be understood by the body, this was an experience, real, literal, in the sense that we as individuals are ever encompassed about by those that are drawn to us by the vibration or attitude concerning conditions that are existent in the experience of entities or souls seeking their way to their Maker. (294-155)

In other words, the experience was not a symbolic but a literal experience, that, indeed, there were entities who came into the church seeking "to know their way to their Maker." As Cayce often said in other readings, when the soul passes over from the physical life, it has merely shed the body; the attitudes and the emotions are still the same as they were on earth. It was the lesson that Cayce was teaching that day that drew those souls in: He was speaking about their own experience. The reading continues:

The carnal eye was then lifted for Cayce, so that he saw . . . As the visions as a child, then, Cayce is again entering that phase of development or experience where there may be in the physical consciousness periods when there may be visioned those [souls] that are seeking in the spirit realm for that which will aid them to understand their relations with the Whole.

Here, the reading is saying that, as time went on, the waking Cayce would have more and more experiences where the spiritual lessons he taught in the material world would be of help to those in the spirit realm and that he would be conscious of such experiences. The reading goes on:

> It should be understood that Life is One, that each soul, each entity is a part of the Whole, able, capable of being one with the Source, or the Universal Power, God, yet capable of being individual, independent entities in their own selves. As He has given, to those whom He calls does He give the power to become the Sons of God.

This point of the reading speaks to each and every soul incarnate on the earth: Each soul is growing, evolving to the place where all of us may become one with God—and that the journey through the earth plane is an important part of that growth and development. Other readings said that, within the three-dimensional world, the soul grows through being patient, being kind, learning to forgive others—in short, learning to love more—and that the more the soul puts these precepts into practice in daily life, the closer the soul grows in awareness with its Maker.

The reading also says that discarnate souls often seek to learn the ways of the spirit from those still in the earth:

> Then, as indicated from that visioned, they that are seeking, though they be in another dimension, or phase, or plane of experience, are listening, harkening, gathering, that they may gain the better concept of what is to be done. Naturally there arise such questions as these: How does a disincarnate entity hear carnally that spoken from a material mind? With what eyes do they see? With what ears do they hear? With what bodies do they appear? Wherewithal are they clothed? As given, "Know, O Israel, the Lord thy God is *one!*" and the hearing that is come, and does come to an entity is with that whereunto the body-entity has builded; hence by the very nature are drawn together as *one*, the eyes as with the visions that are one, whereunto such entities, such souls have seen in their sojourn through the material plane. They are clothed with that body, that clothing which is in its essence from the very source of that builded through the power given them by their relationships to the Creative Forces that are manifest in a material world.

The readings often say that stepping through "God's other door" at the point of physical death is just a step and that there are many more experiences in a life's journey that are more difficult than death. Cayce indicated in this reading that the faculties that we use to hear, see, and feel are actually faculties of the soul, manifested *through* the physical body. When we leave the physical body behind, we still shall have a body. We still shall be clothed. We still shall be able to see and hear. Cayce's reference to the "the Lord thy God is *one*" is a reference to the fact that, that whether the soul is incarnate on the earth or outside of it, it is all one experience. The reading goes on to say:

> That a man's ideas have changed because he has passed from the material plane into the unseen, how can one conceive of this being different? From whence is the lily clothed? From whence comes the clothing that man may wear? From whence comes the power of differentiation in the ability of an individual man to see or to hear? Wherewithal are they given the power to disseminate speech in its various intonations or incantations, for their communications one with another?

Cayce was asking here why we would believe that our thoughts and our feelings would be different merely because we have shed the body? We are still the same in essence, and all power to see and hear comes from a universal, spiritual source—whether we are on the earth or out of it—the very powers that we use in the sensual world come from a spiritual world. Next, the reading says:

> So, as in the vision that is shown here, as in the visions that may come to the body, to the soul-mind of the body, honor and reverence same, that the language of the spheres, that the Voice of the Creative Forces are being manifest; but do not abuse same by *thinking*, acting, speaking or *feeling* that self has been exalted or raised to any particular position other than of being of greater service to thy fellow man. Remember that, "He that would be the greatest among you will be the servant of all."

This reading is saying that Cayce should not consider himself special because he had visions of souls visiting him from the afterlife, but that he should hold such experiences in a state of sacredness and reverence, and he should be humbled by such experiences. The readings are clear that, as we seek to be of help to others, as we pray and meditate, we naturally draw to ourselves not only people in this world who need our help, but also those from other realms and dimensions of consciousness who seek us out for assistance.

There were people who came to Edgar Cayce and asked him about encounters they had with deceased loved ones in dreams and visions. His response to those inquiries was that those souls hadn't come from "on High" to give some sacred message, but that they were seeking the way, the light. And, Cayce said, as we direct those who come to us in visions or dream to the light, so does the way then become easier for us. The following paragraph seems to illustrate that the more we seek to be of help to others, the more will come the opportunities to help others—whether in the body or out of it:

> Know that the body is being given more and more the opportunity then to minister to not only those in the material things in the material life, but these as seen who are seeking in the Borderland, those that are to many a loved one in the spirit land they are seeking—seeking . . .

Cayce often spoke of the *"Borderland,"* a realm of the afterlife where souls are aware of both the material world and the spirit world—a place of the interbetween. As we attune ourselves from within, through prayer and meditation, and as we ask to be a channel of aid, of blessing to our fellow human beings, then the opportunity presents itself more and more for us to be a "light" to those who may be seeking answers, even from the Borderland:

> Keep the faith. Keep the body clean. Look up, *lift* up thine eyes unto the hills from whence the help comes; for God is in His holy temple. Keep, then, thy body *clean*, thine temple of thine body in such a state, *mentally, spiritually*, that He may come and lodge with thee, that He may oft speak with thee as Father to Son. As thine Elder

Brother may He walk with thee in thy going in, thine coming out among men; for that thou hast seen is holy—*holy*; and thou must conduct thine self in such a manner that is *worthy* of these visions, these helps coming to thee the more often. Do not become self-important, nor self-exalting. Be rather selfless, that there may come to all who come under the sound of thy voice, to all that come in thy presence, as they look upon thine countenance, the knowledge and feeling that, indeed this man has been in the presence of his Maker; he has seen the visions of those expanses we all seek to pull the veil aside that we may peer into the future. As ye may become a teacher to those that are "beyond the veil" also, how glorious must be thy words even then to those that falter in their steps day by day!

In patience know thy soul may go out and minister to others. So, as thy presence brings that faith, hope and confidence in men's lives, so may the words of thy mouth be acceptable in the sight of thy Redeemer, so may He indeed give thee the abilities to speak even as the oracles of the fathers, as the oracles of God Himself who sits in His Throne and has given to His Son that ability to quicken the hearts of men that they may know His Face also.

Be, then, patient, my son. Keep in the ways that He has gone. Know that Mother stands near oft, and will guide in the ways that will aid in coming—coming—nearer to the closer walk with Him.

This beautiful passage has a universal message for us all, not just for Edgar Cayce. The readings often reminded people that the job that is of utmost importance in difficult times is to bring hope, light, and encouragement to our fellow human beings. Especially in times of great uncertainty, of global upheaval, of rampant fear, each of us can be a source of light and hope to others by remembering it is the little things that count in life.

As we become such a source, we draw closer to God than we ever could imagine. Edgar Cayce often said that, in daily life, it isn't so important to be good, but to be "good for something!" So often, we are hard on ourselves, reflecting upon our failures and our faults. We should

be turning our thoughts toward the awe-inspiring message of this reading: that, indeed, we can draw closer to our Creator just by being kind
to our fellow man. In our fast-paced, technologically advanced world,
this is a powerful reassurance and reminder for each of us to "remember why we are here"—not for some great accomplishment—although
great accomplishments indeed are done by many. There was a passage
in one reading where Cayce said those who "have saved a soul from sin
. . . have covered a multitude of sins . . . " (262-58) We can interpret the
word *save* in many different ways. From the readings' standpoint, Cayce
would have said it means to make someone feel a little better about
themselves because they encountered us in their lives.

The conclusion of the above reading that says "Know that mother
stands near oft" is very interesting in that it shows the continuing guidance of Edgar Cayce's mother from the other side. Edgar Cayce often
looked to the guidance and counsel of his mother. She encouraged him
during the years of uncertainty, when his psychic abilities frightened
him. She was always a "divine presence" in his life who reassured Edgar
that "By their fruits ye shall know them." In other words, she told her
son that, as long as people were being helped by his psychic readings,
he should continue to give them. Even in his darkest hours, when he
felt unworthy of the gift he had been given, he held fast to the advice of
his mother. In this beautiful closing to the above reading, Edgar was
reassured that his own mother was still looking after him, just as she
had done in her earthly life. At the time of the reading, she had been
dead for five years. We can be sure that our own loved ones, the ones to
whom we look for guidance and assistance, are, indeed, still very much
with us in spirit, and, as we pray for them and with them, we draw
closer to that bond of love that is not material at all, but spiritual and
eternal.

3

Deeper Implications of the Near-Death Experience

A human being is part of a whole, called by us the "Universe," a part limited by time and space. He experiences himself, his thoughts, and feelings, as something separated from the rest—a kind of optical delusion of his consciousness. This delusion is a kind of prison for us, restricting us to our personal desires and to affection for a few persons nearest us. Our task must be to free ourselves from this prison by widening our circles of compassion to embrace all living creatures and the whole of nature in its beauty.

Albert Einstein—*Ideas and Opinions*

*J*n 1980, George Gallup used his polling organization to estimate how many American adults had gone through a near-death experience (NDE). His findings suggested that, by that time, nearly eight million American adults already had had a near-death experience.

"We've learned from numerous studies in America, Europe, and Japan that upwards of sixty percent of patients undergoing cardiac arrest will have a near-death experience happen to them," said pioneering NDE researcher Raymond A. Moody, M.D.[1]

Since the 1975 publication of *Life After Life*, his ground-breaking book about NDEs, Dr. Moody has continued to research thousands of accounts of near-death experiences and after-death communications. Dr. Moody believes that the near-death experience is evolving into a whole new vista of spiritual experience for humanity. The transforming affect an NDE has upon the person who returns from death cannot be underestimated.

"The majority of people who have an NDE return from the experience knowing without question that death is only a passage, not an end," Dr. Moody said. "Further, they return with a renewed sense of spiritual purpose about their lives on earth. It isn't uncommon for people who were primarily material-minded before their death experience to have a kind of spiritual awakening in their values; they return with a *knowing* that above all else kindness, compassion, forgiveness and love are the most important virtues to be cultivated while on earth."

The transforming power of the near-death experience has reached people in unique ways in recent years. Dr. Moody has discovered that another dimension of the NDE seems to be emerging, particularly among Americans born during the "baby boomer years." Dr. Moody has collected hundreds of accounts of a kind of *empathic* near-death experience that he calls *"death coincidents."*

"In these experiences," Dr. Moody has said, "the loved one sitting by the bedside of a dying loved one will *empathically* experience the death transition of the person. There are incredible reports of people seeing the tunnel so often described in near-death experience. Some people see and feel the presence of deceased loved ones, and experience the Light so often described in near-death experiences." In some of the accounts Dr. Moody has collected, people report actually leaving their own body, along *with* the person who is dying, and traveling together through the tunnel, toward the brilliant light.

While in an emergency room with a fellow physician and friend, Dr. Moody actually witnessed a death coincident. The other physician's wife was rushed to the hospital and was in critical condition.

"She was dying," Dr. Moody said, "and they were desperately trying to work on her, to revive her, and my physician friend was standing outside the room. A look of amazement came over his face and he said, 'My wife just passed away. I heard her voice very plainly, and she said, "Good-bye, I have passed . . . " I felt her presence and she is gone now.' [He] experienced the passing of his wife. As soon as he repeated the words his wife had said, the ER physician came out into the hall, and told him his wife had [died]."[2]

It is interesting to note that Dr. Moody's physician friend was not someone with whom he discussed his NDE research, and until his wife's death, the friend had never studied or read material about NDEs. These death coincidents might represent the "next step" in humanity's spiritual evolution toward a broader understanding that the death transition is only that: a transition to another place, where life continues.

"One woman told me she was attempting to resuscitate her mother," Dr. Moody said. "She was frantically trying to bring her mother back when suddenly she felt herself leave her own body, and she rose up and looked down below. She saw herself resuscitating her mother from the viewpoint of being above the room. She was with her mother as they headed for the tunnel with the Light in the distance. It was there she said good-bye to her mother. They did their parting, and she saw her mother go off in the distance, into the light. Then she felt herself get right back in her body." Dr. Moody added that he has heard similar stories from physicians and resuscitating teams, in which they "felt" the person leave the body, and they saw something indescribable, as well.

"I spoke with a television producer sometime ago," Dr. Moody said, "who said she was sitting with her mother while the mother passed away. Her mother started talking to these people who had already died. The daughter looked up *and saw them*, too, and she started conversing with them. Again, I believe this will become as well known and as common as people who have had near-death experiences.[3]"

As time goes on, more of the mysteries of death are being revealed. Death is not, as Shakespeare described it in *Hamlet*: "The undiscover'd country from whose bourn, No traveller returns . . . " Countless travelers have indeed returned and with many tales to tell. One of the things upon which they all agree that is the most profound aspect of their NDEs and the most transforming message to all of us is the simplest: *Love, above all else, is what matters.*

"Upon their return," Dr. Moody has written, "almost all [NDErs] say that love is the most important thing in life. Many say it is why we are here. Most find it the hallmark of happiness and fulfillment, with other values paling beside it."[4]

One NDE survivor who had a near-death experience told author and near-death researcher Kenneth Ring, M.D., how his life had been transformed by his experience. In his comments, there is wisdom for us all:

I realized there are things that every person is sent to earth to realize and learn. For instance, to share more love, to be more loving toward one another. To discover that the most important thing is human relationships and love and not materialistic things. And to realize that every single thing that you do in your life is recorded and that even though you pass it by not thinking at the time, it always comes up later.[5]

What we've done in our lives "comes up later," in what NDE survivors call *the life review*, in which a detailed, panoramic vision of everything the person has ever thought and done is presented in that person's mind or before their eyes. The life review has a profound impact upon NDE survivors because they not only see again every moment of their life, but they also see the events and feel their impact upon others, through the eyes, ears, hearts, and minds of the people with whom they interacted. According to the countless thousands who have returned from death, this multidimensional reexperiencing of life has shown that our words, thoughts, and deeds have far greater impact upon others than we can imagine. There will come a time in each of our lives, after passing from this realm, when we will see and feel how we have made a difference in the world and in the lives of the people we meet day by day—whether that difference was for good or ill.

Many NDE survivors return renewed and inspired because they had no idea, prior to their death experience, of the good they had done in the lives of others. Nor is that good necessarily *deeds* that the world would consider earth-changing. People are shown the importance of the little things, the small acts of kindness and words of encouragement and showing compassion to others. George G. Ritchie, M.D., who died for nine minutes in 1943 as a result of complications from pneumonia, said he saw his good *intentions* as well as his deeds.

"When I meant well for someone," Dr. Ritchie said, "when I just reached out and *desired* to help someone, I saw in my 'review' that *the desire itself was a deed*—it was a thing. The good intention shed light into the life of the person I wanted to help, regardless of whether I was able to do something physically for them. In other words, *the try counts;* the end result has nothing to do with it. The well-meaning intention is a powerful force for good in ways I can't describe. I saw it [in the NDE] as a 'light' of sorts that uplifted the person, and then it lived on and on, and was passed on from that person to countless others. Intentions as well as deeds are like a rock thrown into a pool of water. There is the impact, and then the ripples. Those ripples go through the entire universe. I am convinced that the good intentions people hold in their hearts towards their fellow man is keeping the world intact."[6]

As well as experiencing the good they had done in others' lives, NDE survivors also were shown the pain and sorrow they had caused, seeing and feeling it to the depths of their being, through the eyes of people they had hurt. Many people returned, changed, from their near-death experience because they saw where they had fallen short—they had withheld love or held grudges or were stubborn to forgive others. What made this facet of their experience even more profoundly painful was that, during the life review, they stood in the presence of a completely unconditionally loving being who asked them to examine their lives in terms of how much they had shown unconditional love to others. Near-death survivors said they returned to life with a renewed conviction to heal damaged relationships and to be more loving in both their thoughts and deeds toward others. As one man told Dr. Moody:

> I first was out of my body, above the building, and I could see my body lying there . . . Then it seemed there was a display all around me, and everything in my life just went by for review, you might say. I was really very, very ashamed of a lot of the things that I had experienced . . . That's the part that has stuck with me, because it showed me not only what I had done but even *how what I had done had affected other people.* And it wasn't like I was looking at a movie projector because I could feel these things . . . I found out that not even your thoughts are lost. Every thought was there. [author's italics][7]

Many people return to physical life with a great sense of relief after having experienced this sobering facet of the near–death experience. They very much felt they were being given a second chance. Two people shared with Dr. Moody how urgently they felt the need to be more helpful, more loving toward others:

> I didn't tell anybody about my experience, but when I got back, I had this overwhelming, burning, consuming desire to do something for other people . . . I was so ashamed of all the things that I had done, or hadn't done, in my life. I felt like I had to do it, that it couldn't wait.

> When I got back from this [near-death experience], I had decided I'd better change. I was very repentant. I hadn't been satisfied with the life I had led up to then, so I wanted to start doing better.[8]

One of the most detailed NDEs that illustrates these precepts was chronicled by the Rev. Howard Storm, a United Church of Christ pastor who lives in Cincinnati, Ohio. In 1985, Storm was vacationing in Paris with his wife, Beverly, when he was rushed to a hospital, suffering ex-cruciating abdominal pain. His X-rays revealed a perforation in his duodenum, and Storm was scheduled for surgery. Unfortunately, Storm was in the hospital on a weekend, and only one surgeon was on duty. Nurses were not allowed to administer medication, and so Storm lay dying on a gurney, without even the benefit of pain medication. Slowly but surely, the perforation was leaking blood and hydrochloric acid into his abdominal cavity.

"I kept thinking, this is not how it's supposed to end," Storm wrote. "I was fading away in a Paris hospital and they were indifferent to my agony . . . I was later told by American doctors, back in the United States, that from the time of the perforation my life expectancy was about five hours. The condition I had was similar to a burst appendix."[9]

After Storm had lain on the gurney for ten hours, with no medical attention, a nurse came into his room and announced that the surgeon had gone home and his operation wouldn't take place until the following day. She left his room as quickly as she had come in and Storm, now very close to death, tearfully said good-bye to his wife. She was holding him close and sobbing when he breathed his last. Storm's final thoughts before death came was how tragic it was that this was the end of his life, awareness, and existence. For the better part of his life, Storm had held fast to the idea that, when the body died, life ended. Period.

"I knew for certain there was no such thing as life after death," Storm wrote. "Only simple-minded people believed in that sort of thing. I didn't believe in God, or Heaven, or Hell, or any other fairy tales."[10]

Howard Storm was in for a rude, but much-needed, awakening. It came after he died. He awoke, not realizing he was dead. A chorus of voices called out his name from the hospital corridor, urgently telling Storm to come with them if he wanted help. Bewildered, Storm walked out of his room and found himself following a large crowd of gray, shadowlike beings into a place of ever-increasing darkness and strange fog. Storm kept trying to make out the group's features, but they always walked about ten feet in front of him. When he lagged behind, the beings chastised and berated him, ordering him to keep up. Storm felt no pain, only a deepening sense of despair and dread as the gloom turned into complete and utter darkness. He wrote:

> For a long time I had been walking with my gaze down to watch my step. When I looked around I was horrified . . . we were in complete darkness . . . I told them I would go no further, to leave me alone . . . they shouted and snarled insults . . . they began to push and shove me about . . . a wild frenzy of taunting, screaming, and hitting ensued . . . they bit and tore at me . . . there were dozens or hundreds of them all around and over me . . . Every new assault brought howls of . . . laughter . . . to my horror, I realized that I was being taken apart and eaten alive . . . every sound and every physical sensation registered with horrifying intensity. These creatures were once human beings. The best way I can describe them is to think of the worst imaginable person stripped of every impulse of compassion . . . they were a mob

of beings totally driven by unbridled cruelty ... my torment was their excitement. The more I fought, the greater their thrill ... [11]

Eventually Storm was unable to fight back, and he collapsed in exhaustion. The hellish beings lost interest when Storm stopped screaming and protesting against their cruel assaults. As he lay in the darkness, Storm thought about his old life and where it had brought him. He had lived a life of ego–driven selfishness. He harbored a formidable anger at just about anything and anyone he couldn't control in his life: his father, world injustice, other people. He was virtually friendless and couldn't be bothered with other people's problems. Storm had spent a lifetime cultivating his anger and used it to fuel the illusion of self–protection and self–preservation. As a result, Storm had lived on earth in a state of gnawing inner anxiety, fear, and unhappiness. He dreamed only of becoming a famous artist so he could rise above the people he held in contempt. When Storm found himself in the darkness, he realized all of his life had created the world in which he now found himself. He was alone and stripped of all his selfish defenses, surrounded by beings who held no more compassion for him than he had held for other people during his life on earth.

Storm was experiencing one of the most sobering dimensions of the afterlife: coming face–to–face with himself. The way he had treated others during his life had a direct impact on how he was treated in the afterlife. The well–known Bible verse, "As ye sow, so shall ye reap," takes on a more in–depth meaning when viewed from the perspective of Howard Storm's experience after death.

Lying in the darkness, Storm heard a voice call out to him. The voice was unlike the voices of the shadow–beings. This voice had his best interests at heart.

"Pray to God," the voice said.

Storm hadn't prayed since he was a child and couldn't remember any prayers. The voice was insistent, "Pray to God!" Finally, he mumbled portions of the Lord's Prayer and the Twenty–third Psalm. The shadow beings shrieked and withdrew from him. Storm realized the name of

God was his key to deliverance from the hellish darkness. He called out for help, praying tentatively at first, and, then, with all of his might and being, he cried, "Jesus, save me!" At that point, his path of darkness turned into a path of light. Contrary to the popular belief that Hell is a realm where souls are banished for all eternity and without hope for redemption, Storm *was* redeemed and helped as quickly as he prayed for deliverance. Although he had been shrouded in darkness, Storm came to understand the truth to the words so eloquently written by the Psalmist:

> If I ascend up into heaven, thou art there; if I make my bed in hell, behold, thou art there. If I take the wings of the morning, and dwell in the uttermost parts of the sea, even there shall Thy hand lead me, and Thy right hand shall hold me. If I say, "Surely the darkness shall cover me," even the night shall be light about me.
>
> Psalms 139:8-11

His prayer for help was immediately answered by a being of complete and unconditional love, whom Storm recognized as Jesus. The dazzling brilliance of the His light filled Storm with feelings of complete and unconditional love. Storm's feelings of despair and isolation were forgotten; he was awed and humbled that this powerful presence saw and knew everything Storm had ever thought and done, and still this being loved him completely:

> This loving, luminous being . . . knew me intimately. He knew . . . everything about me. I was unconditionally loved and accepted . . . I experienced love in such intensity that nothing I had ever known before was comparable . . . Jesus *did* indeed love me . . . I had called out to Jesus and He came to rescue me . . . He held me and caressed me like a mother with her baby, like a father with his long lost prodigal son . . . We rose upward, gradually at first, and then, like a rocket, we shot out of that dark and detestable hell . . . I saw a vast area of illumination that looked like a galaxy. In the centre there was

an enormously bright concentration of light . . . While moving toward
the presence of the great light, centre of all being, the One, I was
beyond thought . . . Simply, I knew that God loved me . . . that God
is love . . . This experience of love totally changed my life from the
inside out.[12]

The realm in which Storm then found himself was light–filled, peaceful, joyous. Luminous angelic beings welcomed and embraced him.
Storm wept tears of joy for the redemption and tears of shame for how
far short he had fallen in his life on earth. The reassurance from Jesus
and the angels that all was well, that he was loved and accepted despite
his human failings, was almost beyond Storm's comprehension. He then
conversed with Jesus and the angels, and they answered every question
he asked. When they announced that the time had come for him to
return to his physical body, Storm protested. He didn't want to go back
to his old life and fall into his old patterns of selfishness. The beings of
light assured him they would be watching over him and would guide
him to the right path. It was important for him to go back in order to
share the message of his journey and the message of unconditional
love.

Howard Storm's return to physical life was nothing short of a miracle.
He regained his physical health and left behind his old life as an artist.
Storm came back to life renewed and completely turned his life around.
Today he is a minister, spiritual teacher, and speaker.

The journey from the realm of shadows into the light of unconditional love is a testament to the truth that there is no place in the universe in which God does not exist, even in the darkest, most hellish
realms created by countless thoughts of countless human beings—
ignorant thoughts, selfish thoughts, thoughts of hatred and malice. After death, Howard Storm had gravitated to the realm of shadows that
corresponded to the shadows of selfishness he had cultivated in his
heart during his life on earth. It is interesting to note that, at no time,
did Storm think, "Why did God put me here?" He instinctively knew
that his presence in the darkness was the result of his own doing and

undoing. That realization and his cry for help were the change Storm most needed in order to embrace the light. In order to move from dark-ness to light, we must change our minds, change our hearts.

Although Storm's after-death journey was initially painful, his expe-rience is a lesson to us all on how far-reaching our thoughts, intentions, and deeds are and how they affect not only ourselves, but the people around us. It may sound simplistic to say, "If you would love, show love to others," or "If you would have friends, be friendly to others," but Howard Storm learned from Jesus and the angelic beings that these are spiritual laws and that they are *literally true*:

> "You will find what you look for in people and in the world," they said. "If you are loving, you will find love. If you seek beauty, you will see beauty. If you pursue goodness, you will receive goodness. What you are inside will attract the same from outside. When you love, love comes to you. When you hate, hate finds you."[13]

This law was expressed many times in the readings of Edgar Cayce. He often told people that after death, they would move into a place of consciousness that they had created for themselves, from their lives on earth. The following question and answer for a forty-year-old woman are a good example of Cayce's wisdom on this law:

> (Q): Where do I go from this planet?
> (A): Where thou art preparing, and what thou art building. (1219-1)

Hugh Lynn Cayce, Edgar Cayce's elder son, detailed the readings' philosophy of the nature of heavenly and hellish existence after death.

"Dad put it very distinctly, as I remember it," Hugh Lynn said. "He said that some people are building quite a heaven in their thought patterns and in their way of acting toward others; other people are creating a hell for themselves, and when they die they will have to

move into that state of consciousness, because the attitudes they ha-
bitually express in this life are the ones that they will retain when they
pass over."[14]

Howard Storm's dramatic near-death experience is evidence that,
after death, the soul picks up on the other side right where it leaves off
when it departs the material world. What we have created goes with us
and forms the fabric of our after-death existence. The amount of light
the soul experiences after death has everything to do with how much
light the soul actively sought to manifest during earthly life.

4

Betty and Her Other-World Journeys in the Unobstructed Universe

Life is eternal; and love is immortal; and death is only a horizon; and a horizon is nothing save the limit of our sight.

Rossiter Worthington Raymond

tuart Edward White was a world traveler, explorer, naturalist, and author of more than thirty books, including the bestsellers, *The Blazed Trail* and *The Long Rifle*. In 1919, Stuart and his wife, Betty, embarked on a journey of a vastly different sort, through the unexplored territories of the spirit world. It began when friends brought a Ouija board to a party held at the Whites' home in Burlingame, California.

"Our interest in the Ouija board began quite casually," White wrote. "Some friends had brought it out as a toy to try out, without belief that anything in particular would happen to it. The occasion was derisive and gay. It did not impress me much, but I agreed to try my turn provided my opposite would agree not to fake."

The guests took turns working with the board in twos, and no one was taking it seriously. They would ask silly questions and then laugh when the planchette, the sliding indicator that spells out answers, said "yes" or "no" to their questions.. The laughter subsided, and the party atmosphere turned serious, however, when the planchette quickly spelled out the message, "Why do [you] ask such foolish questions?" Those seated around the Ouija board asked the sitters if they deliberately had manipulated the planchette. No one had. Intrigued, the entire

31

group, except Betty, who was standing by the fireplace, rather bored with the whole affair, sat down to resume the session, their fingers gently resting on the planchette.

"Next our attention was caught by the repeated spelling of the name Betty," White wrote. "We insisted that she was being paged . . . She was reluctant, thinking this merely an attempt of those sitting to lure her back in the game, but finally yielded and took her place."[1]

As soon as Betty's fingers touched the planchette, it zoomed around the board. "Get a pencil," the board spelled out, "get a pencil get a pencil get a pencil." The Ouija session ended there; no one bothered with the pencil for reasons Stuart never detailed. However, several days later, Betty did sit down alone with a pencil poised over a blank sheet of paper and quieted her mind. Within a short time, the pencil began to move very slowly, writing words without spaces, capitalization, or punctuation. Betty knew very little about automatic writing, but she decided to show the curious script to her husband. She assured him that her conscious mind had nothing to do with what was written. They surmised that Betty's subconscious mind had produced the message—even though the message itself said the source of the writing was from a disembodied intelligence.

"It would be silly to adopt such a theory merely because of that claim," White wrote. "It would be equally silly to reject it without further experiment. It would be worse than silly to shy off from the whole subject merely because it was 'uncanny' or 'unnatural.'"[2]

Stuart and Betty began a serious exploration of automatic writing. They agreed to remain both open-minded and discerning and to set boundaries for the experiments. If Betty experienced any ill effects from the automatic writing, either physically or mentally, they would drop the whole thing. They began to have regular writing sessions, during which Betty blindfolded herself or looked away from the paper to keep as much distance as possible between her conscious self and the written scripts. Within a few months, the automatic scripts began to deepen in coherency and clarity, and a purpose revealed itself through the messages received. The writing experiments were a kind of first-step preparation that would expand Betty's consciousness to the point where information of spiritual importance from unseen intelligences could be translated accurately through Betty's subconscious and conscious minds. Betty began to receive mental impressions of the vastness of the real material that was waiting to "come through." She felt it during the sessions and as she read over the material received. According to Betty, the problem was that her conscious mind was a block to or filter of the real information; the messages coming through her were diluted and vague.

"What reached the paper was, according to her, but an unsatisfactory pale shadow of the actuality," Stuart wrote.[3] The Whites then experimented with allowing the spirit guides, whom they called the *"Invisibles,"* to give messages through Betty while she was in a relaxed, reclining position on the couch, in a light trance state. Stuart had read about trance mediumship in the book, *Our Unseen Guest*, and Betty agreed to try the method described by the authors. She lay down with her eyes covered, and Stuart placed his hand on her wrist. Betty easily slipped into a trance, but it took many months before she was able to describe coherently the things she saw and convey messages she heard and received. Stuart acted as stenographer for the sessions, writing down everything Betty said. Progress was slow, and Betty picked up only bits and pieces of information. Stuart said it was like the poor reception received from a flawed radio signal. In order to alleviate the bad reception, the Invisibles said that Betty's mind had to be "expanded" to allow the information to be imparted accurately. Stuart wrote:

> She underwent a continuous and rigorous training as a means to what she called "expansion of spiritual consciousness". She could enter at will a higher consciousness from which she reported back her experiences and what she had seen and was taught. She was able to transmit to me the ideas of discarnate entities we called the Invisibles, either by reporting back as though by dictation or by permitting her speech mechanism to be used directly. These powers and abilities she never used idly, for curiosity, personal satisfaction or any such lesser purposes. She sought and used them to one end only, the expansion of spiritual consciousness.[4]

In many instances of mediumship, a discarnate entity completely inhabits or takes over the medium's body and speaks through the medium's vocal chords. For the entities' work with Betty, this was not the best methodology, according to the invisibles. They said that a co-operative effort was required between Betty and them in order for them to impart the most coherent and accurate version of the information. This involved Betty entering into a trance state and *meeting* with the invisibles in the spiritual dimensions of consciousness they occupied. The invisibles called this intelligent cooperation between the two worlds *the two levels of consciousnesses.* This meant that Betty's consciousness wasn't *taken* from her, but that she would participate in the exchange of information with the invisibles. In short, dialogues took place between Betty and the invisibles from the unseen dimensions, and the information was translated through her voice.

This method was similar to the way Edgar Cayce obtained his psychic information during his readings, except Cayce's conscious mind was completely "asleep" during the sessions. While he was in trance, a part of his subconscious spiritual self traveled through unseen worlds, attuned to the subconscious minds of those seeking help, to discarnate beings or to the heights of the Universal Mind. Regardless of *where* Cayce went or to what source he attuned, the information was relayed through his voice. The difference between Betty White and Edgar Cayce was that Betty retained conscious recall of the places she went, the beings she encountered, what was said during the trance, and how things appeared in the spirit worlds. The purpose of this cooperative work between Betty and the invisibles was to produce a "primer of the after-world"—a body of information detailing the interrelationship between life in the spirit and material worlds and describing the places to which the soul travels after death.

In the early years, Stuart and Betty naturally felt they were venturing into uncharted territory. But they were impressed by the intelligence, coherency, and importance of the information. They intuitively felt their guides were trustworthy and benevolent. Stuart and Betty vowed not to be swayed by the *phenomena* of this unusual undertaking; they kept their eyes upon the *highest ideal:* that the information could be spiritually beneficial and uplifting, as the invisibles said that it would. They remained very level-headed and purposeful in their explorations of the unseen worlds. Subtle changes began to take place as their sessions deepened. White said:

> We must keep the aim single. The primary nature of this aim, also, is very simple: we are headed for the high country of consciousness. If there are such things as "psychic powers," and if we early come into possession of them, it must be for use on our journey and for nothing else. If deliberately we undertake certain initial practices leading to any so-called "psychic state," it will be only as an aid to our greater intention . . . As we penetrate the country beyond, many of these powers and conditions will come to us naturally and securely as a by-product of our progress . . . We must be vigilant neither to strain for their acquisition, nor to abuse the privilege of their possession. For it is when we make them ends in themselves, and collect or develop them for the sake of their power, that they become dangerous. They are staffs for our hands, not stunts for our gratification.[5]

The invisibles cautioned that, as a result of the trance states and involvement with the unseen worlds, Betty would, indeed, become "psychic," and she would have many experiences as a natural byproduct of her attunement to the spiritual realms. Betty's conscious awareness indeed deepened, and she became aware of psychic faculties and abilities that were previously unknown to her.

At the time Stuart and Betty began their spiritual work in March 1919, there was a proliferation of books on psychic phenomena, and interest in spirit communication was booming in America and in Great Britain. The invisibles said that much of the material being brought forth by others concerned itself with superficial communication between the living and so-called dead, but did little else to assist the spiritual faculties of humanity.

"There is too much emphasis on the 'Spirit' aspect," they said, "and too little on the individual application of what it all means. There is too much interest in the mere fact that friends still live about us; overlooking what they come to tell us. Your own growth is what matters. The natural tendency is to seek psychic powers rather than practice human living."[6]

The invisibles were emphatic that *conscious spiritual living in the material world was of paramount importance*. Humanity, they said, had devolved to a point where the masses were not striving to awaken a closer conscious relationship with the Creator. The spiritual stagnation was taking its toll: The world was fragmenting in unprecedented ways.

When Stuart and Betty began their communication with the invisibles, the world was emerging from the trauma of the first World War. It's not surprising that, at times of global crises, there seems to be an increase in spirit communication and spiritual phenomena from diverse sources. Somehow, the messages reach large numbers of people, who are inspired and uplifted by information received from the unseen worlds.

This was certainly true when apparitions of Mary the Blessed Mother appeared to three children in Fatima, Portugal, in 1917. At the time, she prophesied that the war was almost over and that the sons would be returning home. She told the visionaries to tell people to remember to pray—for the children, for peace, for the world. At the same time, Sir Oliver Lodge, whose son was killed in WWI, published a pioneering spiritual book, *Raymond—Examples of the Evidence for Survival of Memory and Affection After Death*. These and other published works about the spirit worlds, the survival of consciousness after death, and messages of divine reassurance, seemed to be an answer to the prayers of a grieving world whose loved ones seemed to be taken too soon.

Stuart and Betty's explorations lent a great deal of light during these troubled times. The invisibles were representative of yet another branch of highly evolved spirit guides who were looking for receptive, open minds in the material world—teachers, professionals, writers—who would assist them in conveying messages asserting the eternal validity of the soul and the need for people to go to the Source, to turn attention to spiritual communion and renewal instead of materialistic diversions. According to the invisibles, the sooner people began to seek spiritual truth, actively and consciously, the better the world would be for everyone on the planet. They said that humanity's collective seeking for "a conscious contact with spiritual truth" must take place at some point in evolution. The world's civilizations literally were falling apart, according to the invisibles, because of the lack of spiritual seeking and contact with the Source.

How did the invisibles propose that people should begin to make spiritual contact? In essence, the principles they outlined were profoundly simple, but profound transformation comes from simple spiritual steps. The first step, according to the invisibles, was *for humanity to contemplate the eternal nature of life itself.* The soul did not begin on earth, nor does it end on earth at physical death. That which is built and those things entertained, sustained, and cultivated in the material world—by individuals and by groups—bears fruit *in both the worlds of earth and spirit.* The essence of that built by the soul goes with it after death. The most important issue the invisibles conveyed through Betty was not unlike the important precept that came through Edgar Cayce's readings: Thoughts and desires are living things. That which the soul cultivates and feeds in its mind and heart, along with the deeds done while on earth, create the soul's home after death.

The invisibles said that one of the first steps to spiritual transforma-tion was for people to desire contact with the spiritual worlds. Desire is a powerful spiritual force. When we have a heartfelt desire to be guided and directed by the Divine Source, or God, and we concentrate upon that desire in prayer or meditation, a powerful vibration goes out from us like a light wave into the atmosphere. The vibratory pattern of desire is an attracting force: It draws to us, from the unseen realms, sublime spiritual vibrations that resonate with our desires. When the desire of our heart is to make spiritual contact with the Divine, we naturally attract spiritual influences of the highest caliber, whose primary interest is the spiritual awakening and quickening of humanity.

Edgar Cayce called these spiritual influences by many names, but he was consistently clear that they were not indifferent forces, but loving, individual entities. He referred to them as the Unseen Forces, guardian angels, spirit guides, messengers from "the throne of Grace, Mercy, and Light." These beings, according to Cayce and Betty's invisibles, are vitally interested in the spiritual quickening and awakening of humanity, and each soul incarnate in the earth has a "friend unseen"—a guardian angel—assigned to them. These unseen friends do not interfere with our free will; they can help us only if we ask for their aid.

Our very thoughts and desires (which Cayce said are literally things) are the powerful inner faculties that put us in harmony with these benevolent guides, and spiritual contact is assured. These unseen beings can (if we will allow them to) carry us from the depths of despair, discouragement, and hopelessness into the light of hope, happiness, and love. The invisibles said, however, that the *conscious* awareness of spiritual resonance is a gradual growth process. We must do first things first. Simply asking for a transformation of thought and desire is a beginning. To help us make spiritual contact, a sincere, heartfelt prayer held regularly is the best way. A simple prayer—such as:

> Dear Lord, Let me this day be in harmony with the Source of all Love, all Light and be a channel of that Love, that Light, to those I meet in every way. Let my thoughts and desires be more and more in attune with Divine Love, now. Amen.

When this prayer is said with sincerity of purpose and intent, it aligns the individual's etheric energy with the benevolent beings who are ever ready to help guide and provide spiritual awakening.

The world in which we live, according to the invisibles, is surrounded by and interpenetrated with powerful spiritual forces. These are not static but intelligent and divinely ordered. Experiencing spiritual contact, they said, is as easy as observing the divine order of nature. They suggested we take a walk in the woods in silence and observe the birds, flowers, and trees. Gaze at beautiful sunrises and sunsets, and let the heart be open. The beginning of a realization of the higher worlds occurs when we open wide the doors of our hearts (not just the mind) and embrace the beauty all around us.

"Until you voluntarily open your spirit to wider influences than those of yourself," the invisibles told Betty, "they could not claim you. By this shift of attention [of focusing on the beauty of the natural world], I do not mean a detailed intellectual appraising of the surroundings . . . I mean simply the expansion that is the result of the shift from a busy mental concentration within to a voluntary wide opening to influence from without. That in itself is a form, a simple form, of spiritual contact."[7]

The purpose of striving for spiritual contact is, in its truest sense, the soul striving for reunion in consciousness with the Creator. In all of the material the invisibles gave through Betty, their emphasis was upon the importance of each soul working to become aware of its divine nature, its unity with the whole of the universe. By seeking conscious contact with the Creator through desire and intention and activity, the soul becomes aware there is a divine "flow" to life, very much like flowing in harmony with the current and direction of a vast river. The invisibles said that many souls who incarnate into the earth become totally immersed in the material world and end up struggling against the current—swimming upstream. Although this is a harder road, the invisibles said there is always growth, always development; but so much more can be accomplished in development of both the individual soul and the world as a whole (because each soul is an integral part of the universe) if the soul will put itself in a position of being guided and directed by the Creative Forces. The invisibles reminded the Whites repeatedly that spiritual contact with the unseen is a return to simplicity: Ask in faith, and you shall receive.

When spiritual contact is sought through deep prayer and meditation, the soul gradually awakens from its materialistic sleep, awareness of being in the divine flow of life dawns, and a more expanded consciousness awakens. The only requirements are consistency and persistency. This broader awareness opens the heart to experiencing a life filled with clarity, compassion, empathy, patience—the "fruits of the spirit." This is where the door opens and the finite self begins to experience the fullness of the infinite. Through time and practice given in expanding the conscious awareness, the faculties of the soul—the psychic faculties—naturally come into conscious manifestation. This is not a strange or otherworldly experience; it is a byproduct of the attunement to the spiritual Source greater than the self.

After many months of spiritual practice and application of the invisibles' tenets, Betty began to be able to report more in-depth mate-

rial about her experiences while in an altered state of consciousness
and began to have many psychic experiences. "In entering this higher
level of consciousness," White wrote, "she has been held, up to now,
rigidly to two purposes; development of accurate reporting ability; and
perception of the specific scheme of truth the Invisibles have determined to impart."[8]

Although Betty was able to retain an awareness of her conscious self
during the trances, her focus of attention was centered not in the living
room, but in the vast expanse of spirit worlds. She was aware of her
interaction and conversations with the invisibles, she was conscious
when the invisibles spoke directly through her, and she had memory of
the information being imparted. Indeed, there was an exchange of information in dialogue among Stuart, the invisibles, and Betty. As time
progressed, Betty felt that she was definitely growing or "expanding" in
consciousness, just as the invisibles said. In the early stages of her jour-
neys, Betty reported she felt like a traveler in a foreign country. A
friendly country to be sure, but it took her some time to become accus-
tomed to learning to navigate her spiritual body while her physical
body was in trance. In short, Betty's comprehension and ability to ma-
neuver with the invisibles in the spiritual worlds required time and
patience on her part. She had to *grow* into her *spiritual* body in the same
way a child gradually learns to crawl, then to walk, then to run in the
physical body.

While she was in the spiritual realms in the early sessions, Betty felt
as if she were being completely cared for by the unseen beings. Betty
was excited about her growth experiences while in trance; as time went
invisibles. She came to understand that her "training" was very similar
to how souls are taught after the death transition. Betty reported that it
was much easier and more natural to move about in the spiritual worlds
than it was in the material world! But there were definite similarities
between the seen and unseen worlds—and Betty was happy to learn
that passing from this world into a world unseen was simply a change
of environment; there was no break in consciousness. When Betty entered into the trance state, she went through what people experience at
physical death. She had no fear or uneasiness during the experience,
and, in fact, there was an exhilaration, a sense of being free when she

was out of body during the sessions. In one session, she described how, in the spirit body, she was able to move from place to place:

> I don't walk. That's a bodily method. I press forward, or something, by a kind of intermittent force of my own volition. I go because I want to go . . . It is smoother than spurts; but it is no more continuous than steps are. When you think of it, it is a current of thought that makes your steps go . . . here [in the spiritual worlds] there's a current of thought that sends you forward—waves of pressure instead of steps. That is what steps are; only here you don't have to have feet for it . . . Now I understand movement. It's the first thing they teach when you go over [at physical death].[9]

It might seem a bit startling to realize that we are "taught" how to move and become mobile in the spirit body after death. Keep in mind that, after many years on the earth, our conscious minds have become focused on maneuvering in a material form, in a material world. After death, we *gradually* let go of that focus, and part of the transitional experience after death is refocusing our consciousness on the faculties of the spiritual body. Edgar Cayce said that our ever-expanding awareness after death is similar to the stages of growth and development we experienced on earth. First, we learn to walk, then run. Then, we are taught how to ride a bicycle, and, eventually, most of us learn how to drive a car. By the time we reach early adulthood, our mind's ability to direct movement via use of the physical body is so deeply patterned as to be automatic. When the thought arises, "I'll walk outside and get the newspaper from the driveway," we simply do it, without much thought or effort. On earth, we come to identify our body as the self, and not simply as the vehicle for the soul.

Although we think of walking, running, and driving as physical, bodily activities, these activities are patterned, formulated, and prompted by the mind. Every activity is a thought before it is a thing or a manifestation. When we leave the body behind at death, the mind and everything that is patterned into it *passes intact* into the spiritual world. In this light, Betty's comment, "It's the first thing they teach when you go over," makes logical sense. Part of the death transition is not merely shedding the physical body—that is only the first stage. There is another transition when the person sheds another body, and that is reorientation to the faculties of the spiritual body.

We might look at the early stages of life after death as a period of "shedding" bodies we no longer need. One of those bodies is the mental body of negative thoughts and beliefs—for instance, inferiority complexes, feelings of insecurity or loneliness, memories of emotional or physical pain, of trauma or suffering, and self-limiting beliefs. These processes are not difficult for most souls. Most are happy to let go of the old thought patterns and negative attitudes. With each passing stage of this letting-go period, the consciousness expands, and there is a pervasive feeling of exhilaration, relief, and happiness. The release from physical form is like a captive bird that is at last set free from the confines of a small cage. As the soul soars free from the old existence, it is in the companionship of spirit guides or "helper spirits." They give encouragement and reassurance to the newly arrived soul and give direction, when needed, for each subsequent step in the soul's journey after death.

Betty's description of these stages of the soul's experience after death is closely paralleled in the book, *Testimony of Light.*[10] Through automatic writing, author Helen Greaves received details of her close friend, Frances Banks', journey through the death transition and her experiences in the afterlife. Frances and Helen were writers in the field of mysticism and psychic and spiritual phenomena. The close bond of friendship they shared on earth continued after Frances died of cancer.

Frances talked about the mental transition phase of letting go of outmoded mental patterns she had built on earth:

> I am like a creature hibernating, and yet at the same time, sloughing off a skin which I no longer will be needing. I feel, sometimes, like a snake gradually shedding its skin. These coils of lower density are slipping away from me. I am emerging from regrets of earth memories, from disillusionment, from idealisations which become illusions, ephemeral and of no true worth. I am viewing each piece of skin which peels off from me in its right connection with the true

Self which it served to obscure. And more and more I become thankful for the Reality which, God be praised, was there beneath the skin, all the time. This is the Self which is now becoming more and more outstanding, more revealed, more substantial. That Self is substantial Light. Perhaps that last sentence rings oddly to you. I am not trying to become obscure, but one's angle of vision alters on this plane of living. I realise that what is passing from me, like sloughing a skin, is insubstantial, impermanent, decomposing, as it drops from me into a dusty nothingness. What is left is essentially Light, is Reality, is permanent and is true. I call this my new Body of Light and that, indeed, is what it truly is. A Body of Light, not dense and material and dull and heavy as the physical body . . . I still have a mind, I still have a body, but both are inevitably changing and because of that I feel as if I am emerging, like a grub from a chrysalis, to a butterfly. Gradually I can function more readily and for deeper periods in my Body of Light, and in it, can commune with more advanced souls and imbibe their wisdom . . . This is the next step in progression, the stepping out of illusion into the consciousness of the functioning of the Higher Self, an emergence into a wider consciousness and awareness of Spiritual Beings and of Forces from the All-Creative Mind of God. This is a gradual process and may take years (in earth consciousness of time) to fulfill . . . The journey itself is compensation enough for the trials of earth existence and for the emotion of judgment in action of those trials and of my individual response to them, from which judgment I am now emerging . . . [11]

In this phase of growth in the afterlife, this "shedding" of which Frances spoke is a death of sorts, but "death" in the sense of letting go of old limitations. Far from being a painful experience, this developmental stage of life after death is exciting, exhilarating, and inspiring. The soul realizes in this state that it is not separate from the Source of all Light and Love, but is a beloved child of the Source, of God. So this is a "death" where this is no grief or sorrow. The soul feels reborn, set free, *released* from the chains of self–loathing, guilt, and other "demons" that hindered or held the soul back during its time on earth.

Betty described the spirit guides important "jobs" of assisting souls through these many transitions. Frances' description of the guides is almost identical to Betty's—but Frances described the job in detail because, after she had made her full transition, she became one of the guides who helps souls who recently cross over. The job of the spirit guides in the borderland at one of the "arrival stations," is to guide the newly arrived soul to a place where it can rest. This is very important if the dying process was long or painful. For example, an elderly person in the last months of physical life and who is no longer able to walk because of crippling pain or illness may pass over very easily, probably during sleep, and is guided to a place of rest, where they awaken in beautiful, serene surroundings. When some awaken, they still believe that they are crippled, and it is the job of the guides to help them "change their minds" and their beliefs so they can see that they are free from the old body. What a joy they must feel when the realization dawns that they've passed into a world where they can move freely and easily—no longer old or crippled, no longer in pain—simply by the power of thought!

There are souls, however, who have a harder time. For the hard-headed materialist who looked out for number one during earthly life or the person who steadfastly refused to believe there is life after death, the transitional experience may be traumatic. It depends upon how stubborn they are. Free will is an eternal faculty of the soul. It is operative during both the earthly life and the afterlife. A soul can refuse to relinquish hold of limiting beliefs, "earthbound" attitudes, or desires, and remain in a shadowy realm of self-imposed exile, refusing the assistance of the spirit guides. They won't be abandoned; they will simply remain in a place between the worlds until they look for the light and ask for help. Just as on earth, it's impossible to help someone who doesn't want to be helped. But Howard Storm's experience is a good illustration of how quickly help can come to the soul, even though it is chained by its own selfishness in darkness.

The stubborn souls who refuse to believe they've died or souls who choose to remain away from the light seem to be in the minority. Most souls who arrive in the place Cayce called "the Borderland" are only too happy to be guided and directed to the next stage of life. The ease with which we pass on to the next phase of our lives after death has much to do with our attitudes and beliefs right now. Betty's invisibles agreed with Cayce that *all spiritual growth attained during earthly life goes with the soul after death* and that growth forms the substance of the spiritual body and the environment the soul will inhabit after death.

Of great importance is how much the soul applied unconditional love and compassion in its relationship to others. There is no judge or jury to balance our faults against our virtues after death; none is needed. Our spiritual body and our mental state of being after death are the sum total of how much we have grown through applying patience, mercy, forgiveness, understanding, tolerance, and other fruits of the spirit to others during earthly life. As we think, so we are. We might even carry this a step further and say, "As we think and act, so we become in the afterlife." In short, the old saying "You can't take it with you when you go," is inaccurate. Whether the "it" refers to the basest of earthly desires or the highest spiritual consciousness attainable, we not only take "it" with us, but since we built "it," it forms the very substance of our spiritual body and our residence. Cayce said, "Like begets like," and "Like attracts like." Under this law, after death, we will gravitate to a place with other souls who are like ourselves, with similar interests, desires, ideals, and intentions. Carefully study the following excerpt from one of Edgar Cayce's readings. He stated that our thoughts and desires imprint themselves into the very atoms and cells of our physical and spirit bodies:

> In the make-up of the active forces of the physical body, it (the body) is constituted of many, many, cells—each with its individual world within itself . . . and when the body is changed [at death], and this is the soul body, the elements as are patterned are of the same. That is, that builded by thought and deed becomes the active particles, atoms, that make up that soul body, see?
>
> When the soul passes, then, from the physical body [at death], it (the soul body) [is] then constituted with those atoms of thought . . . and then we have the soul body, with the mind . . . is . . . the [conscious] mind of the soul body . . . then, we find that as *builded*

by that soul [becomes] the residence of that soul . . . either of the
earthbound or . . . that element, sphere, or plane . . . created in that
soul being in the actions, by the thoughts, of that . . . individual.
(5756-4)

Although Edgar Cayce had no recall of what he said while in trance,
there were occasions when he remembered passing through many levels or planes, where he saw discarnate souls in varying states of growth
and development. In the lower, earthbound realms, Cayce said, some of
the bodies of the people were distorted and exaggerated. These exag-
gerations were created through overindulgence during their earthly life.
He saw souls who had been predisposed or obsessed with spreading
and listening to gossip. Their mouths and ears were larger than any
other part of their body, and the appearance of the individual was like
a caricature. Someone who was gluttonous had a huge, bloated stom-
ach that was so distended, the person could barely move. These beings
would cry to Cayce for help. These visions distressed him, but he knew
he had to continue to follow the shaft of light that guided him during
trance, or else he could get lost. As he traveled, the shadowy forms
gradually gave way to light, and then he saw realms of indescribable
beauty. There, he saw people who were continuing their quest for spiritual growth, souls who desired to be more loving, more forgiving toward their fellow human beings. The bodies of these people reflected
their desires, in radiant form.

Who we are inside ourselves, and what we think, can be hidden
while we are in mortal, physical bodies. After death, we take on the
form of our true selves, and our mental and spiritual selves are revealed.

Stuart White asked the invisibles if the spiritual body was as tangible
as the visible physical form. They responded that it was more real and
indestructible than any form in the visible, physical world. "[The spiritual body] is actually materially that," the invisibles said, "in its own
condition of health and development. It is flesh and it is blood. It may
not be the same kind, but it is as real, as warm, as living as your own."

Betty was able, while the invisibles spoke through her, to stand aside and see the subject matter being discussed. During one session, she described the spiritual body, saying it was "fibreless, but definitely cellular . . . I have a definite body and not a vaporous or fuzzy one either. It is a finer–grained substance than flesh. It is not fluid, but mobile. It is more sensitive, more easily acted upon; and at the same time more indestructible . . . It is a pulsing, living body purified of organic frailty . . . durable, flexible . . . the sense of radius is greatly extended."[12]

Betty had the somewhat unpleasant experience of seeing a realm of disembodied souls who were in crippled spiritual bodies. They resembled human forms, but were gelatinous and spineless, and they shuffled around listlessly in a semiconscious state. This was the realm of souls who were spiritually malnourished, possibly from completely immersing themselves in material–world pursuits without thought of what tomorrow might bring. Cayce said:

> What one thinks continually they become; what one cherishes in their heart and mind they make a part of the pulsation of their heart, through their own blood cells, and build in their own physical [body], that which its spirit and soul must feed upon, *and that with which it will be possessed, when it passes into the realm [after death]* . . . [author's italics] (3744-4)

Stuart White wrote:

> The spiritual body, we are assured, is indestructible. It may be, as Betty saw it, crippled, embryonic, incomplete; but such as it is, it endures. Furthermore, whatever we may add to it in the way of development is an everlasting possession. We may go our ways deliberately blind, deliberately neglectful, willfully procrastinating, self-centered, even antagonistic. These things may form over our real selves a crust that will stop growth. They may act on us, and on others about us, in unguessed ways through long vistas of time. Their effects we will have to liquidate, with compound interest. Their iron

construction we will have to dissolve before again we can expand
. . . Whatever of the spiritual body is in ourselves—even in crudest
embryo—is ours forever, on which sometime or other, when we have
resolved ourselves free, we shall build.[13]

Whether we are aware or not, each day we are building and creating
something that will live on long after we leave this body behind. The
invisibles advised that, the more we are motivated by the heart and
spirit, the closer we grow in attunement to the highest spiritual forces in
the universe. Simply *trying* to show more kindness, more compassion,
more understanding to our fellow human beings accelerates the spiritual growth process by leaps and bounds.

The invisibles were vitally interested in humanity's spiritual awakening on earth. Again and again, they reassured the Whites that the
guardian spirits overseeing the evolution of the human family are ever
ready and waiting to lend a helping hand to take us to the next level of
growth and unfoldment.

What we call "spiritual growth" in the earth is far more real in the
spiritual worlds than we realize. Our spiritual growth and development
are dependent upon how much time is dedicated to deep prayer, meditation, selfless service to others, spiritual studies, and practical application of spiritual laws and truths such as love, forgiveness, patience,
mercy and grace. These "virtues of the spirit" are the building blocks of
the highest spiritual body we will move into after death. Just as no two
people are exactly alike, no two experiences of passing into the afterlife
will be the same either. Each individual's passage into the next world
after death is a very personal, very unique experience for each and
every soul. Although there is truth to the statement that every soul
enters the world the same way (birth) and leaves this world in the same
way (death), the *circumstances and environment* of each soul's occupancy in
the material world and in the hereafter, are as unique as the family into
which it is born.

"It is not a set pattern [after death] any more than birth here is a fixed
pattern," said Hugh Lynn Cayce during one of his many lectures on life

after death. "It's similar, but certainly the birth of a child in the middle of a field in India, whose mother gets up and goes on with the plowing very shortly after, is different from the birth that takes place in a modern hospital here in Virginia Beach. Or the one that is birthed by suggestion or hypnosis is quite different from the one that is knocked out, [or] suffering and screaming, because of lack of knowledge in handling the birth of a child. So it's different here and it's different there, according to the development of the individual . . . We maintain that mental set, that pattern and we carry it over with us. We face the situation we've created. We have the same ideas, the same attitudes."[14]

"First, let it be understood there is a pattern in the material or physical plane of every condition as exists in the . . . spiritual plane," Edgar Cayce said, "for things spiritual and things material are but those same conditions raised to a different condition of the same element . . . " (5756-4)

Life after death is a continuity of the earthly associations and relationships, interests, desires, etc., in the finer worlds of spirit. The invisibles said through Betty that all human beings live together on earth, but all souls exist in uniquely different *levels* of awareness and experience. The endless levels of human experience on earth correspond to endless planes of spiritual existence beyond the three-dimensional world. The invisibles said that the higher the spiritual aspirations and desires to which we hold while in the body on earth, the higher the dimensions of life in the spiritual world with which the soul will make contact—both while incarnate on earth and after death. We don't go to Heaven, we "grow" to Heaven, Edgar Cayce said. This process of growing to Heaven *is not simply a moving upward*, but it is, as the invisibles, said *an expansion outward*. During her sessions, Betty always was attempting to move into the higher realms of the invisibles.

"You have been holding your thoughts and aspirations into a kind of shaft," the invisibles said to Betty, "penetrating, rising above your normal restricted-self senses. Now, having attained a certain degree of light and freedom, you must, like a tree, begin the expansion and utilization. But do not complicate your struggles at present by merely trying to get a sequence further than you have attained. Merely occupy yourself with expanding to your greatest breadth of acute consciousness."[15]

Stuart White said:

> We may define experience as our principal points of contact . . . with
> the outside world. The experience is the raw material that life offers;
> but what we make of it is strictly up to us. If we handle it well we
> make something fine, and our advance is speeded on the road to
> progress. So it is a good thing to know how to meet experience.
> Furthermore, the degree of our ability to deal with it is a pretty good
> indicator of how far we have already traveled . . . In evolution we do
> not advance in company front, but string out irregularly like a crowd
> going to a ball game . . . In the course of our development, we
> progress from one level to another, like going up stairs. And each
> step must be lived out to the full before we can go on to the next.[16]

The invisibles emphasized that, whatever station or place we occupy
in life, the most important thing is to fill that place consciously with all
the love, light, compassion, and patience possible. Edgar Cayce often
said that each soul is as a corpuscle in the body of God. In that light,
wherever we find ourselves in life, we are always in the divine flow of
life and of God, regardless of the outward appearance of things. By
centering our thoughts on the highest spiritual intentions and seeking
to be a light, a channel of blessings to others, we naturally open the
doorway to a greater spiritual awareness, and our consciousness will
expand. In the material world, it's very easy, at times, to fall into a state
of mind that is like being on automatic pilot. We have become so familiar with the daily tasks of our lives that we're not really fully conscious
at all. The invisibles cautioned against falling into this semiconscious
state of "the commonplace," and offered guidance:

> Choose the companionship of inspiration wherever it feeds and
> nourishes, whether in the gift of dead poets or the sweating toil of
> living workers. Outside your hours of duty refresh and stimulate your
> thought chambers by constantly associating yourself with the
> aristocracy of the spirit wherever you can recognize it. There is

always such a drag to the commonplace, such a vortex of it. You must continually guard yourself against it if you are going to maintain yourself above it. I am not saying there is anything wrong about it: I am only saying it is crowded. Our restricted imaginations, our semi-paralyzed wills, our spasmodic instead of habitual acknowledgment of the unknown—by all these we keep ourselves commonplace . . . Do not mistake us, we do not worry about your application to little necessary things—it is the *unbroken* application. That's the thing that makes you commonplace. If you stop work, even drudgery, often enough to switch your center of consciousness to big spiritual proportions, you can accomplish ordinary life without getting commonplace. You must get outside of a thing, always, to recognize it. So keep alternating your centers of consciousness frequently enough to get a proper proportion.[17]

In 1939, after thirty-five years of marriage and twenty-years of spiritual exploration with the invisibles, Betty died. Because of the vast amount of time she had spent in the spirit worlds, she faced her own death with a great sense of peace and talked about her transition as one would talk about preparing for a great adventure.

"For years, Betty had been running back and forth to the other consciousness as easily and naturally as a cat in and out of a house," Stuart wrote. " . . . that she should face her final transition to this consciousness with serenity, then, was only to be expected."[18]

Stuart White didn't experience a deep sense of loss or grief after Betty's passing. On numerous occasions after her death, Stuart experienced many instances where he felt Betty's vibrant presence sitting next to him, "the cozy, intimate feeling of companionship you get sometimes when you are in the same room, perhaps each reading a book." The love he felt from her and for her had not diminished simply because she had passed through the veil to another stage of life. Betty was, for all intents and purposes, focused in another dimension of the universe, but she still occupied the same universe as her husband. The invisibles often said there are two perceptions of the one universe:

the "obstructed" and the "unobstructed."

" . . . in its two phases of Obstructed and the Unobstructed," Stuart wrote, "the former being life as we know it here on earth, and the latter life as she [Betty] knows it beyond earth. There is, actually, only one universe, says Betty, and death is but the throwing off of the earth's obstructions . . . "[19]

We might think of it in terms of our three-dimensional world (obstructed) being a projected reflection of the infinite spiritual world (unobstructed), out of which all life springs. The obstructed is where we go to school, and the unobstructed is our eternal home. When Betty died, she graduated from school and went "home." The bond of love Stuart and Betty shared for many years was just as real once Betty had "thrown off earth's obstructions":

> . . . within a few minutes [after Betty's death] . . . [the awareness of our togetherness] flooded through my whole being from Betty, but in an intensity and purity of which I had previously had no conception . . . I have never in my life been so filled with pure happiness. No despair; no devastation; just a deeper happiness than I have experienced with her ever before . . . and furthermore it has lasted, and is with me always . . . Betty had not gone . . . The presence has continued, not all the time, but normally so. I go into a room; she may or may not be there. I stroll about her garden; she may or may not walk with me. But many times throughout each twenty-four-hour-day she is there, her vivid personality enveloping me.[20]

Perhaps the many years they had spent exploring the worlds of spirit together brought Stuart and Betty closer in spirit after Betty's death. Stuart felt Betty as more tangibly present than he had ever experienced before. This doesn't mean that Betty was an earthbound spirit. Betty was going on with her life in other realms, but her passing did not signify an end to the spiritual bond she shared with Stuart. Perhaps the difference between Stuart and others who grieve over a spouse's passage is the *degree of sensitivity* Stuart had for the spiritual side of life. He was attuned to the spirit realms as a result of the work he did with his wife for many years. Naturally, that spiritual work built a spiritual or psychic awareness that transcended the so-called boundaries between the material and spirit worlds, and Stuart was able to feel his wife, and the love they shared, more deeply than ever before. It was a full and fruitful life. Stuart felt that the twenty years he and Betty worked with the invisibles were the most intimate years of their lives. Between 1919 and 1939, they amassed a collection of 2,300 typewritten pages of dialogues between Betty and the invisibles, which resulted in four published works.

At the time of Betty's death, Stuart didn't realize that Betty still had more to say. Her physical passing did not signal the end of the work with Stuart and the invisibles. Six months after her transition, Betty communicated through her close friend, Joan (pseudonym), the psychically gifted medium who, with her husband, Darby (pseudonym), authored the book, *Our Unseen Guest*. Stuart, Betty, and Joan had done some spiritual work together years prior to Betty's passing, in which they conducted psychic experiments to prove the reality of the "beta" or spiritual body. Although they hadn't seen one another frequently over the years, Betty felt a close spiritual kinship with Joan.

"In spite of so few meetings," Stuart wrote, "the two of them [Betty and Joan] had always 'clicked.' And they always felt that . . . they were destined to do more good work together. But they, no more than Darby or myself, realized how perfectly they were being trained, each in her own way, to combine their methods in one triumphant effort when the time came."[21] That time came in the fall of 1939, when Stuart visited Darby and Joan on the East Coast.

Joan agreed to go into a trance and try to contact Betty. Within moments of Joan's entering the trance state, Betty made her presence known. Stuart was awestruck because the cadence and rhythm of Joan's voice were "pure Betty." Betty mentioned not one, but dozens of small events out of their past. She spoke of little anecdotes and recalled many endearing moments she and Stuart had shared together. Many of the things of which Betty spoke were gone from Stuart's memory, until Betty brought them up again.

Betty's purpose in speaking of the little things was to validate for

Stuart that it was, indeed, his wife speaking. Because of the intimate nature of the subjects of which she spoke, Stuart was convinced beyond any doubt that it was his beloved Betty. Then she got down to business. Betty's communication wasn't merely for the purpose of returning to "speaking terms" with her husband and close friends. Betty also returned to give information that would help other people who are bereaved and those who feared death and to answer some of the so-called "unanswerable questions" about what happens to the soul after death. Thus, the work Stuart and Betty had conducted for twenty years continued. Now, however, Betty spoke from the vantage point of being a resident in the unobstructed universe, not a visitor, as she had been during her earthly life. Because of her close relationship with Joan, the information she imparted through Joan was very lucid and remarkably undiluted. In short, Betty's unique individuality was just as apparent to everyone in the room as it had been when she occupied a physical body. Betty spoke of death as being *a change of perspective* and reiterated that the passage is but another stage of growth and development for the soul.

Betty said:

> The world calls me . . . dead. But sometimes people, unable to endure the thought of such a blanking out, speak of a loved one as having "gone on." That idea, *the act of going on,* is more correctly true. It is true that we are "changed;" but so is man in his earth experience changed from a new-born child to adulthood. And not only is he changed physically, but his perceptions are changed . . . It is so that I am changed—so all we "dead," are changed; glorified with our own immortality . . . We have indeed gone on beyond the comprehension of your present earth perception; but so is man beyond the comprehension—even the sight perception—of that new-born child. Of course it takes only a little while before a baby begins . . . 'to notice.' It is the same with you. You, the World—so small a child in Time's duration of the Universe—only notice us as yet. But just as the noticing of a child brings a feeling of personal comfort and stability back to him, so would the world's acceptance of Immortality bring back stability and comfort to mankind . . . only by a re-

establishment of the old faith in the continuity . . . the purpose and responsibility of life—that people or nations can regain stability. *Stability* is what you have lost and are now seeking to regain. Not security. Security is material. Stability is spiritual.[22]

Betty's message struck a chord with everyone present. The world at that time knew very little of stability: It was 1939, and the turmoil of World War II was adversely affecting everyone. Betty's definition of stability as a spiritual state of being was enlightening. When queried further, Betty said that the old order of things had collapsed. The same elements that had brought about the catastrophe of World War I were now aligning to bring about even further devastation.

"What brought about this collapse?" Stuart asked.

"Loss of faith in the present fact of immortality," Betty replied.[23]

Stuart added:

[Betty] does not mean . . . a conscious attitude of agnosticism or denial. We may still profess belief in a vague and remote 'heaven' to which eventually we shall go. But belief is not faith; and it is *only faith*—faith in the same sense that we accept the inevitability of death itself—that can transfer the field of our practical endeavor out of the present moment. When the present moment—the earth span of life—is all that concerns us, then the emphasis of all we think and all we do at once bases on materialism. More and more we have been tending toward writing off everything but the gain of the day. We deny the claim of the future; we are increasingly indifferent to the coming generations. We are emphasizing *rights* rather than *obligations;* those obligations that a real faith in immortality must impose.[24]

Stuart and Betty's comments echo what Edgar Cayce said prior to the U.S. involvement in World War II. When the earthly span of life, or the "world of appearances" is all that concerns humanity, then the motivating influence behind the thoughts and activities of the masses is strictly materially driven. The higher spiritual aspirations are forgotten, and the laws of the jungle becoming the ruling influences. Hence, chaos and collapse become imminent because, without a spiritual foundation, no earthly "building" can stand for long. Our present society is not far removed from what the world was passing through back in 1939. We are living in uncertainty and fear from the threat of terrorism; tensions in the Middle East seem to be building to yet another breaking point. Some of America's largest corporations, that were once the benchmark of financial stability and security, are collapsing. Many companies, where people once could work to retirement and with a pension almost guaranteed, have closed their doors or laid off employees and relocated to countries outside of the U.S. In uncertain times, when nothing in the material world can provide a sense of "safe haven," where can we turn?

In 1939, Edgar Cayce gave a reading on world affairs that correlated with Betty and Stuart's view that the world's problems begin when humanity looks to the material world as its "god" and elements of spiritual faith are ignored. Cayce said:

> The cause of strife now and of that which will be a part of America's experience lies in unbelief. The very [dwelling of] thought upon those things that are at variance to the principles of right, justice, mercy, peace, the right to worship according to the dictates of conscience, as thought is given we find that power to the thought is created by the very mass of the thought itself, as well as conditions that become individual problems in the lives of the peoples of America.
>
> Yet as we find, if there is the turning of every man and woman to the thought of God, then we may solve every problem. For it is not by mere thought, not by any activity other than the moving force within each entity, each body; and when more of patience, more tolerance, more thought of others is advanced and kept in the heart of the individual, this lends that power, that influence, that force for good. (3976-24)

Betty's advice and counsel from her "unobstructed" perspective sheds a similar light upon the cause of world instability. That advice, just as is the wisdom of the Cayce readings, is as applicable today, in the twenty-first century, as it was in 1939:

> When humankind gets far enough away from the fact of immortality, it has to come back. Or perish. And the only way it can come back is to *cease looking outside itself and search within* [author's emphasis]. Furthermore, any coming back always means a new pattern. Recognition [that] the Creator [is] greater than the thing created. Realization that man's thoughts and activities are a real and vital part of the scheme of things, having their effect on the Whole as well as on himself. Not only here and now, in his own little segment of the universe, but on out in an eternal continuity. Immortality![25]

The foundation of all things in the material world springs from the spiritual Source. Is it any wonder that chaos and collapse occur when masses of people have more faith in the thing created than in the unseen spiritual Source—the Creator—Who brought the material universe into manifestation? In order for us to survive and prosper in uncertain and unstable times, we must return to "first things first." To people who sought him out for a reading, Edgar Cayce often posed the question, "In Whom, in what, do you believe?" If our highest spiritual aspirations ascend no higher than our material selves or material goals, without faith in a spiritual Force, then whatever is "built" materially has no foundation upon which to stand.

Seeking counsel from the Divine within, consciously seeking to align the small self with the greater Self, which is unseen, is an active step toward *faith-full* living. Looking to the outside world for the answers to the world's problems brings nothing but more confusion, more chaos. The outside world is the realm of the *effect*. When we look for logical answers to problems, without respect to the *realm of cause*, our purpose is defeated. Confusion and further chaos naturally will result because the outside world has no answers that will satisfy the inner longing of the soul, which is a longing for spiritual communion with the Source from which the soul came. In meditation and prayer, the self seeks beyond the material world of appearances for help from the *spiritual Source*, or God. To live life with a belief in immortality, as Betty said, is to take into account more than "living for the moment;" it is living an expansive existence that takes account of other people and "tomorrow."

An extreme example of living without a belief in immortality might be a group of people or a large corporation that makes the decision to dump toxic waste into a river or the ocean. Instead of taking into consideration the far-reaching destructive effects such an act will have in the future, the deed is done with thought for only the present moment, with an attitude of, "A hundred years from now, I won't be around, so who cares?" This kind of destructive activity blatantly ignores tomorrow. There are thousands of scenarios such as this one, in which choices made by individuals, groups, or nations are made without thought of the future. Perhaps the vast environmental problems the world suffers today are an accumulation of hundreds of years of acts done without regard or respect for immortality.

Problems are brought into being not only because of deeds, but also because of *thoughts*, which are *things* in the mental realm that one day must find expression in the material world. There are many destructive forces that have been unleashed because only the "short haul" was considered and there is no concern for how people in the next generation would be adversely impacted. In this light, separateness is chosen as the ideal instead of oneness. By natural consequence of breaking spiritual law, chaos and instability manifest in the material world at the mass level, due to disregard for what Betty called "faith in immortality."

An absence of this faith also adversely affects the world from the attitudes and beliefs held in the mental realms. Each individual's thoughts, feelings, and actions impact and affect the whole of the universe itself. If we dwell upon despair and hold no hope for the future, then despair and hopelessness will come into manifestation in our individual lives and also will manifest somewhere in the material world. When one person looks beyond the mundane concerns of earthly existence, and opens the door to spiritual renewal, ripples of light go out from that individual and touch and uplift the individual and the universe. On the other side of the coin, the darker attitudes and emotions such as despair, hopelessness, and fear also have a ripple effect, casting shadows throughout the world that make it difficult for the light of love, peace, and harmony to manifest. But, Betty reminded Stuart, each individual holds within self the vast power to be of help and hope to the world *en masse*. No act of kindness, no good intention is ever wasted; a positive thought for the future, held in prayer or meditation, contributes immensely to opening the door for light to come in where there was once only darkness. Although we cannot see these things at the material level, in the spiritual dimensions, prayer and meditation for peace are the most powerful forces aiding individuals, groups, and nations.

Stuart and Joan continued to communicate with Betty through the early 1940s. As the casualties mounted in 1940 and 1941, during the dark days of World War II, Betty shed some light in a discourse describing her work on the other side with soldiers who were killed in battles:

> Well, first of all, we have to find one who speaks the language of the newly arrived soldier. It is a mistake to imagine that merely coming here enables us to speak and understand all languages. We don't. Suppose the newly arrived is a Russian. He is met by someone who speaks Russian, who not only speaks to him in his language, but surrounds him with the vision of familiar things . . . You must remember that most of them [new arrivals after death] do not know what has happened to them. They probably think that they have been wounded or stunned, and that now they are in some new rest area. Most of them argue that as they can see and hear and are not under the ground, therefore they are [still on earth].[26]

For those who die unexpectedly or violently, every effort is made for the incoming soul to have as peaceful an experience as possible. The soul awakens, after the passage from the body, in familiar surroundings, with no memory of the traumatic events that led up to death. Betty said that the great majority of souls she attended were taken to a large hospital or care center, where they could adjust gradually to having made the transition.

" . . . a great many require treatment," Betty said. "For instance, a man who has been hit thinks he is without one leg. That thought must be cured here, just as the leg would have to be treated . . . in one of your hospitals. Here is where we treat and care for such . . . disabilities."[27] The astral realms attained immediately after death are a place where what one believes and thinks becomes a reality. So, the higher evolved spirit guides (some of whom were once human beings such as Betty) help the newly arrived soul to learn how to *think in terms of wholeness.* For example, someone who dies from cancer might awaken, still believing they are sick. There are beings present at the awakening of that soul to assure it that it is now healthy and completely free from illness. As quickly as the soul can open to this "healthy thinking," just as quickly, their body follows suit and is immediately well.

The recuperative realm is the place where the soul receives instruction and guidance from the spirit guides on how to let go of earthly thought patterns and beliefs. Each new arrival has a compassionate spirit guide, which we might call a guardian angel, assigned to them. The guide's job is to make the death transition as smooth as possible. The time it takes to fully comprehend being in the afterlife is different for every soul. Most souls are happily surprised to awaken and realize they "survived" death and are still intact! Some souls, however, take the news of their death with some degree of turmoil. Betty explained:

> In the case of some, when finally they realize they are dead, they become uncontrollably hysterical. We then induce sleep . . . There are places for them [the soldiers who died in war] where there is nothing but peace. There each is given a *vision* of the future, of what the sacrifice he has made is going to mean to the world; what his contribution has been; how much better the world will be because of it. And to this place each brings whatever is his contribution for this peace. For instance, right now there is a group of Russian soldiers who have brought music. And the others bring whatever they have that can make pleasure—the enjoyments of life.[28]

The "vision" of which Betty spoke refers to a portion of the life review, that near universal part of near–death experiences. In Betty's description, the life review shows the soul how the future was positively
affected by their selfless efforts. So the review of one's life is not only
about the past, but also about how the activities, thoughts, and intentions of their earthly existence continue to uplift and benefit the world
and countless souls in the future. This is another example of the ripple
effect: The good we try to do for our fellow human beings today ripples
out and continues to positively affect many, many people for many
tomorrows to come. It is also inspiring to know that the talents we
cultivate on the earth—whether music, art, writing, or some other special ability—go with us after death. Nothing is lost in the transition.

Betty also described how part of her work with soldiers involved
bringing the soldier's family members and friends to the other side during sleep. The
Cayce readings say that, when we dream of a deceased friend or loved
one, real contact is made. An informal poll[29] showed that approximately
twenty–five out of 100 people who have experienced the death of a
companion, best friend, or close relative will have, within a three–month
period, a vivid dream experience of the deceased. Most of those reported that the dream was more vivid or emotional than other dreams.
Betty explained it this way:

> During the night, we are sometimes able, while they sleep, to bring
> parents, wives, sweethearts to their loved ones here . . . We brought
> a woman who is still there, in the [earth], to her daughter, who is
> here. The daughter had been a nurse, and she was killed . . . the night
> we brought the mother, in her sleep, this girl insisted she must have
> on a nurse's uniform. When the time came for the mother to go back
> she did not want to go . . . she . . . begged to stay here with her
> daughter . . . she was so frantic that finally we had to put her to sleep
> here to induce her to go back; and we did not leave her until she was
> safely back.[30]

Upon waking from the dream experience, the mother did not recall "begging to stay" or being in a frantic state. What she remembered was how real the dream felt, how close her daughter felt to her and how very alive the daughter seemed. From the moment the woman awoke from this after-death encounter with her daughter, the mother's feelings of grief and loss rapidly dissipated. Recalling this dream filled the mother with peace. From Betty's description of this vital work, we now have a deeper understanding of dream encounters with the deceased: Such experiences may very well be orchestrated by the spirit guides and our loved ones from the other side. The more open-minded we are to having such experiences (and we should not be surprised at having such experiences after a loved one passes), the more our minds are attuned and aligned with the invisibles who are anxiously waiting to help us move into a more expansive understanding about the oneness of life and death.

Edgar Cayce said there is a very close relationship between the sleep state and the death state: " . . . sleep is a shadow of, that intermission in earth's experience of, that state called death . . . " (5754-1)

At death, we leave the body for good. In sleep, we leave our bodies at night and return in the morning. We may not be conscious of it, but the subconscious mind is in attunement with other subconscious minds. When we pass from this world after physical death or when we go to sleep at night, the subconscious mind becomes the conscious mind of the soul. The subconscious mind forms a bridge between the worlds and a natural avenue to communicate, through dreams, with our deceased loved ones. Instead of viewing such experiences as strange or out-of-the ordinary, we should anticipate and look forward to having such beautiful "dream reunions." The natural state of the soul's awareness is that it knows no division between the worlds. In the conscious state, we've been taught that, when someone dies, they are gone, and as we think, so our reality becomes.

We can heal the sense of loss and bereavement by having a "life review" before going to sleep at night, remembering the wonderful moments we shared with a special friend or family member who has passed. Instead of focusing on their being gone, why not do a little experiment before you go to sleep: Close your eyes, and call from your memory some of the happiest times you shared. Do your best to silence the voice of grief that wants to interrupt your life review to say, "Those times will never come again." First and foremost, *that is not true.* Go back now, and do your best not to just remember, but also to relive the funniest, the best, the most heartfelt moments you shared with your loved one. Drift off to sleep with those treasured memories in your conscious mind, and *know in your heart that you will share times such as those again.* Further, expect to see and talk with that beloved friend or companion when the time is right for the both of you. Don't be surprised if that very night you find yourself in a happy dream, reminiscing with your friend. Look forward to it. Be excited about it, just as you would be excited about an earthly reunion.

As stated earlier, everything that exists in the material world was a thought before it was a thing. After death, in the realm of the astral world, that which is thought, believed, or desired by the soul immediately becomes manifested as a reality. An in-depth understanding of this power is of paramount importance in the first stages of life after the death transition. Recall, for instance, Betty's story about the soldier who had died with a missing leg. In the realm of recuperation, his having two healthy, working legs was only a *matter of his belief,* but he had to be taught how his thinking directly influenced his condition. In the recuperation realm that Betty oversaw, what we believe is what we are. As quickly as the soul changes its mind from thinking, "I am sick," to, "I am healed," just as quickly is that change manifested in reality.

Even in the material world, we are the sum of all that we have thought and believed. Although there doesn't appear to be an immediate change in the physical reality when we change our minds, eventually the resulting physical reality will indeed change. Having a broader spiritual life in the material world begins, first and foremost, with our minds, our thoughts, and what we believe. Norman Vincent Peale spent a lifetime teaching people the immense power that exists in positive thinking. His motto was, "If you can believe it, you can achieve it." Any positive advancement in life—whether in the physical world or in the spirit—begins with expanding the horizons of the mind's beliefs and desires.

Betty repeatedly told Stuart that there is only one universe. There are no barriers that separate the seen from the unseen worlds. The illusion of separateness is based upon the world of appearances. We appear to be separate individuals because we cannot see the spiritual bond that unites us all. In the Western world, we have become so enmeshed into the material world that we doubt the reality of anything that cannot be seen or touched. When it comes to dealing with issues of death and dying, the Western world has long held the belief that death is the end. This thinking, according to Betty, is viewed as a sad state of affairs by souls who have passed on and by the higher beings who are overseeing humanity's spiritual evolution:

> There is no genuine separation, and the only unhappy barrier that can be interposed between yourselves and those who have [passed] on . . . is undue grief carried to the point of desolation. That interposes a barrier. Your dear ones understand perfectly, of course, how natural it is that you grieve. But the very closeness of the tie brings us [it is Betty telling this, from her vantage point] a complete awareness of your grief; and it must make us sad to see you suffering. *Those on this side do not suffer or sorrow as you do there* [author's italics] . . . But we must share your sadness when you grieve so much . . . If you want to contribute something to us, do something for us, keep away from undue depression and grief. That is one positive thing you can do for us. You can at least avoid casting a shadow on our new estate.[31]

From Betty's message, it is evident that our loved ones are clearly aware of our thoughts and feelings after they pass. If for no other reason than that, we should cultivate healthier attitudes about life and death for our loved ones's sake. Our prolonged grief adversely affects the soul on the other side. It "casts shadows," as Betty said. If we take the time to work toward replacing our feelings of loss with something more hopeful and positive, a whole new spiritual awareness is waiting to be born in us. We shut the door to spiritual awakening and experience when, for example, we say, "Well, she's gone. I don't know what I'll do without her. I wish I hadn't said [. . .]; I never told her I loved her . . . "

Keeping in mind the premise that thoughts are things, how else could such "things" as these impact our loved ones on the other side than painfully? What are such limiting beliefs creating in our lives? Regret, guilt, feelings of separation, isolation, and loneliness.

To begin to heal such a sense of loss and bereavement, we must begin with our own thoughts and beliefs and *repattern our thinking*. Our minds operate very much like a computer. What we program into it by thought gets printed out into our lives. The old thought patterns and beliefs we've held for a long time don't just go away; they need to be replaced or reprogrammed. When feelings arise at the thought that, "She's gone," patiently sit quietly and come up with a thought or affirmation that will open the door for healing: "She has passed on to a new life. She knows how much I love her; she is aware of the love we shared and the happiness we knew together. We will meet again because love is eternal and so are we." We should meditate upon these new thoughts. As often as the old thoughts come crashing in, we must patiently persist in replacing them. After a time, the feelings of loss and loneliness naturally will begin to dissipate because the new thoughts take root and take the place of the old. The positive affirmations we use align us with a higher spiritual reality than we are conscious of at present. Through time and persistence, the more we dwell upon the continuity of life and not the separateness of death, the more spiritual truth will gradually unfold in our consciousness, and the more continuity of life beyond death will be not just belief, but also something that we *know* with every fiber of our beings.

Since thoughts bring realities into being, we can be sure—we can have faith—that our positive thoughts will bring us greater reassurance and greater peace than we ever could have imagined. First and foremost, however, we must have the desire to transcend the limiting belief in loss—and embrace something higher, something that we cannot see or feel, but in which we can have faith that, through turning our attention within, we will come to know and experience the full truth that nothing we have loved is ever lost.

We often ponder where our loved ones go after death. We use terms such as "the other side" and "heaven" because, in the material world, we perceive one another in terms of space—in terms of here or there. "If I am here, then you are there." With this thought construct, it's very difficult to fathom Betty's assertion that there is "only one universe." Betty attempted to explain this to a visitor who sat in on a Joan–Betty session. She was always averse to references to herself as if she were some disembodied, floating, vague form. She described herself, passionately, as "still human!":

> "What is your idea of where I am now, anyway?" Betty asked a visitor . . .
>
> "Why . . . " stammered the visitor, "I just think of you as suspended, somewhere, in space."
>
> "I am right here," she was most emphatic . . . "It is only that you can't see me; can't hear me, unless the talent of someone like Joan lets me express myself through it."
>
> "'I have thought of you as a higher octave. Are you always near us?" the visitor asked.
>
> "'Where else would I be?" Betty responded. " . . . Suppose you were on a mountain. You could see the clouds below you. They have form, color, substance, and they screen from your sight everything below you. Yet you are aware that there is a world of action below the clouds. To the bodily you, and to your actual knowledge, those clouds are no obstruction. They are an obstruction to only one of your five senses—vision. You can eliminate that by . . . the act of walking down the mountain path . . . It is only that my I-Am is separated from the obstruction that was my body . . . "[32]

We might think of the obstructed universe as a stage within a theater. Upon this stage are all the props of our material lives. Upon this stage is played the drama of our lives. The set is so believable that, after a time, the actors forget they are playing a part—and even forget they are in a theater. So focused are the actors on the script and unfolding drama, how could they possibly conceive of the theater, let alone a world outside of the stage? Death is when the actors relinquish their costumes and leave the confines of both the stage and theater, finding themselves in wide-open spaces—the unobstructed universe outside of the props. Suddenly, their experience becomes so much more expansive—because, when they look up they see not the fabricated scenery of the sky inside the theater but the *real* stars—they see the broad expanse of life outside the illusion of the theater. Then memory returns, and the actors come to realize that the so-called solid reality of the material world was not only *not* the true reality, but it was, in fact, a projection or an image of a greater reality. Life in the obstructed universe is important, for what is learned through interacting with other "actors" goes with the person who leaves the theater and has great impact on the next stage of life in the greater, expansive worlds of the spirit.

5

Spiritual Masters, the Elders, and the Great White Brotherhood

Human beings are but a single manifestation of the Infinite Creator. Besides them are hosts of ascending Forms intent upon final unification within the spirit of the Eternal Maker. To learn of these myriad expressions of God's life adds breadth, depth, and loftiness to our thoughts.

Flower A. Newhouse—*Natives of Eternity*

*I*t is evident that, while Edgar Cayce was in a trance giving psychic readings, he was not acting alone; the information that came through him was the result of a group effort. When giving a health reading, the first words he spoke after receiving the hypnotic suggestion from the conductor of the readings (usually his wife Gertrude) were, "Yes, we have the body . . . " When the reading was to obtain spiritual advice, he would say, "Yes, we have the information . . . " If a past–life reading was sought, Edgar Cayce would say, "Yes, we are given the records of the entity . . . yes, we have information before us."

Who, exactly, were the *we* of the readings?

The answer to that question is complex because, when he was in a trance, Cayce's subconscious soul–mind operated like a finely tuned radio receiver. Based on the suggestion that was read to him as he entered the self–induced unconscious state, Cayce was able to attune to an infinite number of psychic sources of information. In the collection of 14,305 documented readings that have been preserved, catalogued, and indexed since his death in 1945, Cayce gave detailed answers on some

10,000 subjects. Two-thirds of those readings were health readings. Physicians who worked with Cayce learned very early that, if their patients followed the suggestions and prepared any prescriptions or obtained any treatments exactly as Cayce described them, the patients generally regained their health. Obviously, the unseen beings who called themselves "we" in Cayce's readings were very wise and very adept at helping Cayce retrieve information on any subject about which he was asked.

> When Dad would give a medical reading," Hugh Lynn Cayce said, "it was like listening to a medical professor giving a dissertation from *Gray's Anatomy*. Those readings were so detailed I have no doubt that Dad was working with a group of physicians on the Other Side to give the proper diagnosis and prescriptions. It was a matter of attunement, you see—the suggestion for physical or mental or spiritual information sent his [Edgar Cayce's] mind to the subconscious mind of the person who was seeking help. From there, his soul-mind was attuned to the person who needed help, and with other beings who were very adept in medical knowledge. In other readings, Dad was able to give detailed information from the past, on ancient civilizations, etc . . . again, he was in tune with another group of beings as well as the Akashic records—a kind of vast universal memory bank in which everything that has ever happened on earth is recorded upon [what Edgar called] 'the skein of time and space.' The readings themselves said Dad's subconscious mind was amenable to suggestion while in an unconscious state.[1]

That amenability to suggestion was an important part of Edgar Cayce's psychic ability. But there was another important factor that determined the accuracy of the information received: *the sincere seeking of the person or group who requested the reading.* If the seeker were sincere in the desire for help—whether from a physical or a spiritual reading—that determined Cayce's ability to attune to the information and the "unseen forces" for the information requested. Hugh Lynn Cayce said that, if someone were wishy–washy, didn't believe in the readings, or was just seeking information out of curiosity, then the information in the readings might be vague or even incorrect.

In 1919, Edgar Cayce prepared a list of questions for Gertrude to ask him during his trance about his psychic ability to give readings and about the accuracy of the information given:

> [Edgar Cayce] obtains . . . information from that which it has gathered, either from other subconscious minds . . . or from minds that have passed into the Beyond, which leave their impressions and are brought in touch by the power of the suggestion. What is known to one subconscious mind or soul is known to another, whether conscious of the fact or not . . .
>
> (Q): Is this information always correct?
>
> (A): Correct in so far as the suggestion is in the proper channel or in accord with the action of subconscious or soul matter . . .
>
> (254-2)

So, Edgar Cayce was drawing from the subconscious minds of the reading recipients, but he was also in touch with *other beings* who had, as Cayce put it, "passed into the Beyond . . . " It was a group effort, and there were occasions when the attunement of an individual or group was so perfect, through sincerity of purpose, that the information came from the highest spiritual sources.

In the records, there are occasion where the divine sources of the Most High—we might call them adepts, masters, archangels, or the elders—actually made their identities known in the readings. In one of the most profoundly inspiring passages ever given in the readings, the source of the message was even identified as the Master Jesus. This might seem hard for some to believe, but remember that Cayce's sincere goal and ideal in life were to use his psychic gifts to be help humanity. By the end of his life, Edgar Cayce had read the Bible through sixty-seven times. He was devout in his faith, and he consciously looked to Jesus, the Master Soul, for guidance and direction in his life. In his psychic work, Edgar Cayce prayed that the Master would protect him from interfering "forces" and help provide information that would be of benefit—physically, mentally, and spiritually—to everyone who sought Cayce out for a reading. As he looked to Jesus in faith, and when the people surrounding him during the reading did the same, then it was only natural that the Master himself would make His presence known in the readings.

In July 1929, Edgar Cayce was giving a reading on his psychic work. Questions were posed to him on how best to carry forward the information so that people could be helped. It was during this reading that the attunement was in perfect accord with the Most High, and this awe-inspiring message was given, urging all the people involved with Cayce's psychic work to work cooperatively and harmoniously:

> In these things, then, let each be mindful of that place, that niche . . . each is to fill, and *fill* that with *all* of the power, might, strength, that lies within that body! So cooperate with other individuals, working in their individual capacities, that the whole purport [standard] may be as one, even as the Father and I are one in you. I speak not of myself, but that ye may know the truth, even as delivered in the day when I walked among men and became known as the Son of Man, and the Savior of a benighted race. Here, my brethren, ye are come again to fulfill, in this place, a glorious principle, a glorious article of work among the sons of man. Let each, then . . . become one in purpose. (254-50)

The waking Edgar Cayce was deeply moved and humbled by this message, and he was naturally very shy to discuss it with even his closest family members. He often went off alone to pray and read his Bible after such inspiring messages were given through him. Dr. Harmon Bro, a psychologist and theologian who spent a year living with the Cayce family in 1943–1944, recalled overhearing Edgar Cayce in prayer, after word was received that one of his readings helped restore the health of a little girl. Cayce's voice was trembling with emotion, as he said, "Thank

you Father, thank you for all good and perfect gifts we have received . . . I
of myself can do nothing; all glory and praise is thine . . . thank you for
using this lowly channel to bring healing to those who seek . . . "

When someone was healed as a result of his psychic readings or a
message came through him from an archangel or other messenger of
the Most High, there was no one who was more awed than Cayce himself. Remember that he was unconscious when he gave his readings; he
had no conscious recall of anything that was said while he was in trance.
Edgar Cayce was grateful that help came through him and that divine
reassurances were given in his psychic readings because he, like all of
us, was very human. Edgar Cayce wrestled with the "things of the flesh."
He had frailties, weaknesses, and temptations just like everyone else. So
he held all the more fast to his faith in God and prayed that his mortal
limitations would not interfere with the information that came through
him in the readings.

In 1933, Cayce provided some of his own conscious insights about
the sources of his psychic information during an informal talk given at
an open meeting of his spiritual study group in Norfolk, Virginia:

> As to the validity of the information that comes through me when
> I sleep, this, naturally, is the question that occurs to everyone.
> Personally, I feel that its validity depends largely on how much faith
> or confidence the one seeking has in the source of information . . .
> With regard to the source of information, I have some ideas,
> naturally; but even though I have been doing this work for thirty-one
> years I know very little about it . . . I, too, am only groping. But then,
> we all learn only by experience. We come to have faith or understand-
> ing by taking one step at a time. We don't all have the experience of
> getting religion all at once, like the man who got it halfway between
> the bottom of the well and the top when he was blown out by an
> explosion of dynamite.
>
> As a matter of fact there would seem to be not only one, but
> several sources of information that I tap when in this sleeping
> condition. One source is, apparently, the record that an individual
> or entity makes in all its experiences through what we call time
> . . . The sum-total of the experiences of that soul is 'written,' so to

speak, in the subconscious of that individual as well as in what is known as the Akashic Records. Anyone may read these records if he can attune himself properly. Apparently I am one of the few who can lay aside their own personalities sufficiently to allow their souls to make this attunement to this universal source of knowledge—but I say this without any desire to brag about it . . .

Some people think that the information coming through me is given by some departed personality who wants to communicate with them, or some benevolent spirit or physician from the Other Side. This may sometimes be the case though in general I am not a "medium" in that sense of the term. However, if a person comes seeking that kind of contact and information, I believe he receives it . . .

So I believe that if the source is not wavered by the desires of the individual seeking the reading, it will be from the Universal. Of course, if an individual's desire is very intense to have a communication from Grandpa, Uncle, or some great soul, the contact is directed that way, and that becomes the source. Do not think that I am discrediting those who seek in that way. If you're willing to receive what Uncle Joe has to say, that's what you get; if you're willing to depend on a more universal source, that's what you get. "What ye ask ye shall receive" is a two-edged sword. It cuts both ways.[2]

Edgar Cayce encouraged people who sought him out for a reading to desire help from the Highest. In the readings themselves, the advice was the same: Seek for the universal knowledge and wisdom, and seek for nothing less than the Most High.

In 1935, members of a spiritual study group in Virginia Beach, Virginia, sought information of a very high spiritual source. Their opening suggestion to Edgar Cayce, as he entered the trance state, directed his unconscious mind to a plane where the highest spiritual information could be obtained:

The members of the Executive Committee of Group 9 of the A.R.E
. . . Salute Thee with Greeting of Deepest Love and thank Thee for
again bringing us the Ministry of our Kind and Helping leader, Edgar
Cayce . . . we hereby petition your indulgence and cooperation in
bringing to us the following information, as questions are asked, for
the more perfect functioning of the work of Edgar Cayce and the
Association from this time on, if same meets with your pleasure to
do so. (254-83)

After repeating the suggestion aloud, Edgar Cayce then obviously
attuned to a group of beings of the Most high. His voice, according to
one who was present for this reading, took on a commanding, powerful
tone, the vibrations of which made all present feel they were in the
presence of a very holy, very spiritual "group" of beings:

Yes, we—from the source of all knowledge that is promised in Him
salute thee, and give that which will be helpful to those who seek to
be in the ministry of those influences and forces that make for more
and more awareness of the divine in each and every soul, that—
applied in the experience of each entity, each soul—will bring that
day of the Lord that is at hand to those who will hear His voice. Then,
*from the heights of those experiences, those hierarchies in the earth
and in the air, we come as messengers of truth to those who will hear,
and question.* [author's italics]

(Q): To what extent are the Masters of the Great White Brotherhood directing the activities of Edgar Cayce? Who are the Masters
directly in charge?

(A): *Messengers* from the higher forces that may manifest from the
Throne of Grace itself . . . Those that are directed by the Lord of lords,
the King of kings, Him that came that ye might be one with the
Father. (254-83)

The Great White Brotherhood is a group of unseen beings, spiritual masters who help direct spiritual awakening in individuals, groups, and nations of the earth. (The word *white* is a reference to the white light of the Christ, not to race.) Edgar Cayce was attuned to these high messengers, as indicated when he said, " . . . as from those hierarchies in the earth and in the air, we come as messengers of truth to those who will hear, and question." (254–83) As evidenced by this statement, these highly evolved beings are involved with both incarnate souls on earth and souls who have passed on. In the same reading, the group asked about Edgar Cayce's involvement with the Great White Brotherhood:

(Q): If Mr. Cayce is a member and a messenger of the Great White Brotherhood, how do the *Masters* wish him to proceed and should not his activities henceforth be presented as Their Work?

(A): As the work of the *Master* of masters, that may be presented when in those lines, those accords necessary through the White Brotherhood . . . Let the light of Him, thy Christ, thy God, in, that it may cleanse thy body, that it may lighten thy soul, that it may purge thy mind, that ye will only be just gentle, just kind; not find fault with any, for with faults ye build *barriers* to thine own soul's enlightenment. "I, thy God, thy Christ, beseech thee!" (254-83)

Again, the emphasis is upon the *attunement*. The reading is saying that the members of the brotherhood are a source of information in the readings "when in those lines, those accords necessary . . . " But the reading advises that those seeking help and divine aid should seek the Highest, the "*Master* of masters." It isn't through some magical ritual or some esoteric mantra that individuals may attune to the masters, the elders of the brotherhood, and the Master Himself. It is simply by persistent seeking within through prayer and meditation, by being kind, by showing compassion, by being less judgmental. It is in the seeking and the asking for direction and aid, asking to be used as a channel of blessings, asking to be of help to others daily that we draw closer to those unseen forces Cayce called "messengers from the throne of Grace,

Mercy, and Light." Through time and patience, we will be made aware of the benevolent spiritual guides, for these divine messengers of the Most High are cognizant of human beings, anxious and willing to help humanity make the next evolutionary step in spiritual awakening.

The Great White Brotherhood also figured prominently in the work of Russian spiritualist Madame Helena Petrovna Blavatsky, founder of The Theosophical Society in 1875. The term *Theosophy* was formed by combining the Greek words for God and wisdom. Mme. Blavatsky authored many books, including *Isis Unveiled* and *The Secret Doctrine*. These exhaustive volumes explored the astral realms, reincarnation, universal laws such as karma, and the origin and destiny of humanity. The society set up headquarters in India and gained a huge following. Some of the more well-known Theosophists were Thomas Edison, Alfred Lord Tennyson, and William Butler Yeats. Two of the leading authors and speakers of the Theosophical movement in the late nineteenth and early twentieth centuries were Annie Besant and C.W. Leadbeater. Both were gifted with clairvoyance and the ability to commune with the Masters, the adepts of the Great White Brotherhood.

Leadbeater wrote:

> Students of occultism, even those who have been students for many years—sometimes seem to fail to realise the Masters as They truly are. I have often found people thinking of them as some kind of angels or devas, or . . . as so far removed from us by Their greatness that is scarcely possible for us to derive much help from Them . . . They are very close to us, so that Their sympathy and help are very near and very real . . . [The members of the Brotherhood] may be divided into two classes—those who retain physical bodies, and those who do not. The latter . . . hold themselves suspended . . . between this world and nirvana, and They devote the whole of Their time and energy to the generation of spiritual force for the benefit of mankind. This force They pour into what may be described as a reservoir, upon which the Masters and their pupils can draw for the assistance of Their work with humanity . . . [3]

Leadbeater said that the brotherhood are beings who have advanced in spiritual evolution to the point where they are free from the necessity of reincarnation. Although free from the material world, they selflessly choose to work, as Edgar Cayce described, within "those hierarchies of the earth and of the air." One of the ways in which they have helped humanity is the legacy of the Edgar Cayce readings. Within those readings are answers to life's most enigmatic questions, and there is spiritual solace, comfort, and wisdom for those seeking spiritual truth and direction. This is one of the areas in which the brotherhood acts on behalf of humanity: They renew the spiritual truths, generation after generation, through the introduction of various religious and spiritual organizations, and they work through gifted seers and mystics. Leadbeater spoke of how human beings work in tandem with the brotherhood:

> Tiny though our efforts may be . . . we also can add our little drops to the great store of force in that reservoir. Every outpouring of affection or devotion produces a double result—one upon the being to whom it is sent, and another upon ourselves, who sent it forth. But if the devotion or affection be utterly without the slightest thought of self, it brings in its train a third result also . . . devotion or affection of the truly unselfish [individual] moves in an open curve, and though some of its affects inevitably react upon the sender, the grandest and noblest part of its force ascends to the Logos Himself, and the response, the magnificent response of benediction which instantly pours forth from Him, falls into that reservoir for the helping of mankind. So that it is within the power of every one of us, even the weakest and the poorest, to help the world in this most beautiful manner. It is this adding to the reservoir of spiritual force . . . [4]

Where Leadbeater used the terms "devotion and affection," we can use the example of prayer as a means for helping our fellow human beings. When we, in earnestness and sincerity, pray for world peace, those prayers reach the Divine and then go into the vast "spiritual reservoir." There, those prayers become literal forces for shedding light where there is darkness, harmony where there was only chaos. Once again, we are back to *intentionality*—our intentions are deeds. When we, in kindness and selflessness, open our hearts and try to be more compassionate, forgiving, understanding to our fellow human beings, we are then aligned with those of the holy brotherhood. Edgar Cayce said a handful of people sincerely praying and meditating for peace have *saved entire nations* from destruction. No kind thought or deed is ever wasted, regardless of the outward appearance. This is where faith comes in; although we may not see immediate results from our "affection and devotion," we must have faith in the vast power the individual has to change and better the world.

The brotherhood ultimately is directed by the Creator, ever yearning for Its creations to turn from darkness to face the light and remember the truth: Each human being is a child of the universe—eternal, undying, and loved completely.

In October 1935, Edgar Cayce had a visionary experience just before entering the sleep state to give a reading for a forty-five-year old woman who had requested a mental–spiritual reading. Cayce saw the woman's spiritual mentor and recognized him as one of the Great White Brotherhood. The mentor was dressed in a very white robe and white turban. After Cayce described the spirit entity to the woman, she decided to ask about Cayce's vision in a subsequent reading:

(Q): What relation did the experience had by Edgar Cayce, of seeing a mentor at the period of my last reading, have with my development. Give name if possible.

(A): Here we have a most holy experience. Keep inviolate, my child, those things that must shortly come to thee, if ye will but harken to the voices within. *This* again is indeed him that *proclaimed* that the day of the Lord *is* at hand—John. It is indicated in the very manner of his garb; as of one clothed and his raiment shall be white as snow, and they whose sins have been as crimson shall be washed and as wool. His feet are not of clay; his feet are not as brass, but as of gold—that bespeaks of the endearing messages that may be brought to thee and thine, that thou may indeed, *now, fulfill* that for which *then* thou didst dedicate thy life; that ye through thine efforts in flesh may proclaim the wondrous year of the Lord for men!

(Q): What relation of John to the White Brotherhood?

(A): As then, the leader; now among the head of the Brotherhood.

(587-6)

Mrs. [587] was a very spiritually evolved individual. She was involved with many facets of Edgar Cayce's work, and she was working particularly on developing her spiritual gifts as a healer. It is fascinating to note that the entity known biblically as John the Baptist was now the head of the brotherhood and was assisting in the spiritual development of both individuals and groups. Leadbeater said the same in his book, *The Inner Life:*

> Then the one who was once the disciple of Jesus stands ready especially to guide the various activities of the Christians . . . [5]

In 1943, a sixty–eight–year–old man asked Edgar Cayce what he must do to be able to be in communication with the members of the brotherhood:

(Q): Will I be able *consciously* to communicate with Masters of the Brotherhood in this incarnation? If so, is there anything I can do to develop that ability?

(A): If the self is purified of every selfish motive, and if the seeking is that such be given that it may be administered to warn His people. But if it is only for the gratifying of self, no. Possible then, and probable, if the self will sanctify thyself in purpose, in body, in mind.

(Q): Is it likely that I will meet any of the brothers in the flesh in this incarnation?

(A): Ye may meet many. For, oft doth man entertain angels
unawares. (3011-3)

Members of the brotherhood not only are working "behind the
scenes" in the lives of human beings, but also, according to the above
reading, they can manifest in the flesh. Leadbeater said these evolved
beings can take on physical form and appear as ordinary human beings
when the need arises. There are also masters who do incarnate and live
among people. Cayce often told people to be kind to strangers, to passersby, to those we might not know but who may need our help. In some
cases, these strangers, who might appear average or even as a homeless
person, are there as tests in our lives—to see how compassionate, how
kind, how willing to be of service we truly are.

In one story about St. Francis of Assisi, the patron saint of animals
and nature, he was walking down the road with his disciples. Coming
in the opposite direction was a leper. The disciples steered clear of the
man, while St. Francis went over to the man, embraced him, and said a
prayer and blessing over him. The leper thanked St. Francis for his kindness and continued hobbling his way down the road. St. Francis' disciples were uncertain what to say or do, but he showed them
compassion for not wanting to get near the man and told them that
they needed to be kind to all passersby, because (as Cayce said, and as it
is written in the Bible), we often entertain angels unaware. St. Francis
then directed his disciples' attention down the road to where the leper
was walking. When they looked in his direction, the leper turned around
and, suddenly, his countenance changed: He was a light being who
looked like Jesus! The being smiled and raised his hand in a blessing to
St. Francis and his disciples. Then, just as quickly as the glowing white
countenance had appeared, the being became again a leper and returned to hobbling down the road. On the road of life, we can never be
sure whom we will run across in our day–to–day existence: a master, an
angel, or maybe even the Master Himself!

Although we use the term *brotherhood*, this doesn't in anyway exclude
women, and the brotherhood works in all nations and through all reli-

gions. Many women who received readings from Edgar Cayce were told that they were guided and directed by those of the Great White Brotherhood; some were told that they were members of that order, even while incarnate in the flesh. In 1935, a forty-eight-year-old woman was given the inspiring message in her life reading that she was indeed one of the Great White Brotherhood:

> For, as in those [past lifetimes] the entity gained the greater, so may those influences come in the present to make for the opening of self for the higher influences; and the sons of light as from the holy mount guide thee in thy walks and thy meditations, for thou *art* of that Brotherhood! (812-1)

In the late 1800s, there was a young boy who was gifted with clair-voyant vision, and he kept a diary of his amazing psychic encounters. He was able to see through the veil of the material world and communicate with his dead grandfather. He also was able to communicate with members of the Great White Brotherhood. His spirit guide was one of them, and he called this guide "the Elder Brother" or "E.B." for short. The boy's diary was published after his death as *The Boy Who Saw True*, but only upon condition of anonymity. To this day, the identity of one of the most psychically gifted persons ever documented has never been revealed.

The boy could see and hear entities in the spiritual dimensions as easily as we can converse with one another in the material world. He could read minds, could see auras and nature spirits (called gnomes, fairies, etc.), and spoke with scores of so-called "dead" people—some of whom didn't realize they were dead. At the tender age of ten, however, the boy didn't realize that other people didn't have clairvoyant sight as he did. In an early diary entry, dated July 8, 1885, the young lad wrote about seeing spirits and of trying to reconcile the more traditional views Christianity had laid out regarding Heaven and his own experiences of talking with his dead relatives. The parenthetical notes below were added by the diarist as an adult, as he prepared the diaries for publication:

When I hear music, I see lovely things and sort of have the most lovely dreams. I am sure there must be a lot of music in heaven, though I don't believe people sit all day and play on harps, else how could I have seen Uncle Willie and Grandpa and the like. [Both were deceased at the time of the writing.] They didn't have harps—and come to that—they didn't have wings either like pictures of angels in the goody-goody books. Georgina (the cook) . . . says that when good people die, they are turned at once into angels, and sit round God singing hymns for ever and ever. But how could she go and say that when she must have seen people (spirits) who weren't sitting around God? (I had still failed to grasp that everyone could not see spirits, or better said, was not possessed of "astral sight.")[6]

It wasn't until the boy became acquainted with his private tutor, a Mr. Patmore, that he realized he saw and heard much more—with his psychic senses—than the average person. He was quite adept at telepathy and could pick up the thoughts of people with whom he was conversing. He telepathically picked up on Patmore's memories with astonishing accuracy. The teacher was, naturally, awed and was amazed even further when his long-dead best friend appeared to the boy and gave him a message for Patmore:

Today we had geography . . . and we'd been looking at a map of Canada, and Mr. Patmore told me he'd been there once . . . I was in one of my knowing moods this morning, so while he was drinking his milk I said, "You won't be cross if I tell you something?" And he promised that he wouldn't. So I said, "When you were on that big boat going to Canada, you got sweet on a young lady, didn't you? and thought you'd like her for your Mrs. But After you got to Canada . . . when you did see her again, you got . . . disappointed, and thought you wouldn't fancy her as your Mrs. after all." Mr. Patmore . . . said, "Well, I'm jiggered. How the Dickens did you know that? I'd almost forgotten about it myself." So I said I didn't know how I knew, but that it just comes to me. He seemed as if he couldn't get over it, and said, "Well, that's most extraordinary. I've never believed in second sight, but I think you must have it. Can you tell me any more?" I was going to say no, when I saw (the spirit of) a rum looking man ... and he said, "Ask him if he remembers Sam North, and the scrape we got into that day." So I asked him, and he [was] ... more surprised and said, "Don't I remember him indeed. He was one of the best fellows I ever met ... he saved my life that day." "Well," I said, "there he is now. Can't you see him?" "Go on with you," he said, half laughing, "of course I can't see him. I only wish I could." This seemed to please Mr. Sam North so much that he pulled a jolly face, and said, "Tell him he'll see me all right when he gets over here."[7]

This was the first psychic experience between the boy and his tutor, and it was the beginning of a lifelong friendship. While editing his diaries for publication, the author wrote a side note saying that the above incident was a very important turning point in his life because it was the first inkling he had that he was "different" because of his clairvoyance.

"I had at length found out indirectly through my tutor," he wrote, "and the incident above related, that my faculties were peculiar to myself, or at least, were not possessed by everyone. This becomes apparent later ... Mr. Patmore was ... impressed by my sensing to set about studying the claims of Spiritualism, and in the end became quite a convinced spiritualist, though at the time, I myself had never even heard of the cult or its phenomena."[8]

Mr. and Mrs. Patmore took the boy on holidays, and these getaways offered many opportunities to explore the boy's psychic abilities. The boy's dead grandfather would answer questions asked by the Patmores, about life on the other side. The grandfather proved to be extremely entertaining. The Patmores also conversed with members of the brotherhood and with the boy's guardian, E.B. The grandfather told the lad that the coming together of Patmore and the boy was orchestrated from the spiritual realms by the boy's deceased grandfather and the elders. Prior to meeting Patmore, the boy had been under an abusive teacher in school; he was close to having ulcers and was suffering other physical problems. The grandfather had told the boy that he soon would be seeing a doctor and instructed him to tell the doctor everything about the cruel school teacher. The grandfather had said it was very important that the boy do so, so that *they* (the grandfather and the elders) could arrange for the boy to be taught at home by a sympathetic, open-minded teacher who would provide the boy with a fine education, as well as assist in him expanding his psychic abilities.

"Cheer up, my lad," the grandfather said, "*we* are looking after you, and soon you will hear there will be no more school."[9]

Sure enough, the boy followed his grandfather's instructions, and from the other side, arrangements were made to have Mr. Patmore be the boy's teacher and mentor.

Although most of us may not be able to see or communicate consciously with the other side as the young boy did, as we pray and meditate to be divinely guided, we will be "prompted," through our intuition, in the direction we should go. Every human being is guided to some extent by the guardians and spirits from the other side. One example of the evidence of this is those peculiar, positive "coincidences" that arise when we meet the right person at the right time. Although many people call this a "lucky break" or a matter of chance, these events in our lives are literally divinely ordered—there is no such thing as chance when it comes to those coincidental meetings and happenings in our lives that lead to our betterment.

Each soul, according to Edgar Cayce, has a guardian spirit, and these are sent by the Creator, who is cognizant of each soul. The more we look to the Divine for aid, the more that God can send the messengers, the elders, to intervene in our lives in the most extraordinary ways. When a "coincidental meeting" happens that is of benefit, we should always pause and give thanks to the Creator for lovingly assisting us. Although the little boy's clairvoyant experiences may seem unusual to us, out of the realm of our experience, his synchronistic meeting with a teacher who would become his spiritual mentor should remind us to look back at the times in our lives when similar events have happened. It may have been when we met the person with whom we fell in love. It may have been when the perfect job just dropped into our lap, or when we were in dire straits financially and, suddenly, the money we needed "just showed up." These are not, by any means, events of chance or luck. These are evidences of divine intervention. The more we have an "attitude of gratitude" about such events, the more in harmony and in tune our lives will become. If we *expect* our lives to be divinely led and guided, then by the power of our desire, sincerity, selfless intention, and faith, God opens the door for this to become a reality. In other words, we can all be led by the elders, the masters, and the Master Himself.

As the boy grew older, his clairvoyant abilities also expanded. At the end of World War I, he gave readings for people whose sons had been killed in battle. He kept in contact with Patmore and kept him abreast of all of his activities. When they could, the two got together and had sessions with the elders, who gave inspiring messages about world circumstances and the nature of life after death and answered their questions. Patmore served as stenographer during these sessions, and the young man repeated the words of his grandfather, other spirits, and members of the brotherhood who came to speak with them. The grandfather was very wise and told the young man and Patmore that the grandfather was continuing to learn and grow since his physical death. He said that, after death, there are wonderful places to go and compassionate teachers who teach souls about spiritual laws, the importance of love, and an infinite number of other subjects in which souls are interested.

On September 19, 1888, the boy wrote about his grandfather coming to them and giving a beautiful discourse on the nature of love. The way the boy wrote about his grandfather's message is beautiful because it shows the boy's innocence and happy personality, which makes the spiritual essence of the truths he describes all the more heartfelt:

> Yesterday Grandpa came and gave us [a] talking to about love. He says in the spirit world it's love what counts, and the grand people there are not the folk what used to be dukes and duchesses and Sirs and Ladies, but the people who shine the most with the light of love. He said we ought to try and feel loving to every one, be they ever so humble or ever so wicked, then we shall be all the happier on earth and ever so happy when we get to spiritland. He said . . . love is the

most beautiful thing in the world. He says it is love that holds the world together, and if God was not Love, the world would all go to smithereens. He told us that when we meet some bodies we don't like, we should say inside ourselves, "Peace be with you," many times, and after that we'll feel quite different about them. He said he was sorry he hadn't loved more bodies when he was in our world, but he'd had it knocked into his head that you can't have many friends, and can never be fond of a lot of people, but only a very few. Grandpa says now that's all fiddledeedee and that when people can't be fond of a lot of folk it's simply because they haven't much love in their hearts, and can't see the good in others. He says it's often just a silly pride that makes people like that, and they ought to be learn to be more humble and feel kindly towards every one. Good old grandpa!

After the boy had kept the diary for a year, his grandfather urged him to keep writing down the messages from the other side because it would one day benefit many, many people. Since the diaries were first published in 1953, they have been reprinted fourteen times. The latter part of the book contains many messages from the elders, transcribed by either the diarist or Patmore.

At age eleven, the boy began receiving spiritual instruction from higher members of the Great White Brotherhood. Before falling asleep one night, the boy saw a master standing at his bedside:

I was longing to see the E.B. again, it seems so long since he has been [here]. Last night while I was cogitating in bed, I saw a spirit with a lovely aura but a queer kind of face a bit like a Chinese doll but much nicer. He stood at the foot of my bed and smiled ever so sweetly but said nothing. I wonder who he is and what he wanted? I have a feeling he will come again.[10]

Indeed, the master the boy had seen did come again while the boy was with Patmore. The master was introduced by the E.B., who first gave a them both a spiritual message. He told them that each soul who is consciously treading the path of what the E.B. called "spiritual knowledge" has two teachers. The E.B. was one of the boy's teachers, and the other teacher was the spirit the boy had seen at his bedside. The E.B. called this teacher "the Lama" and said he was alive on earth and occupied a "Tibetan body." The E.B. would not disclose the Lama's name, but said with earnestness and sincerity:

> Love us both . . . not because we demand love for ourselves, but because love is a force which we can use for good. Love is also a bridge which spans the unseen. On the wings of love, your mind may fly to us in its bewilderment and receive its answer . . . it is not always possible [for us] to come when your heart desires our presence. Nevertheless, our voices may be heard by those who know how to listen. And so, when there is a problem that frets you, think of us forcibly with love . . . and listen with your inner self, and you will receive the answer . . . [11]

These are instructions that can benefit us all. When the E.B. said the guides' voices can be heard by those who "know how to listen," he was referring to meditation. It is sometimes difficult to quiet the mind and enter the stillness in this chaotic, fast-paced world. Now more than ever, however, if there is a barrier or a veil between the material world and the unseen worlds of light and wisdom, where the Great White Brotherhood resides, it is thin indeed. The masters urgently want to guide humanity toward greater enlightenment. We need only enter the silence of meditation each day; to know, with reverence and without question, that we are entering the "secret place of the Most High;" and to have faith that we will receive the answers to problems. We will be given the strength to go on when the road of life becomes rocky. We will hear the divine voice that says, "All is well. Be at peace," and we *will* be at peace. In order to have this experience, we must pay the price of diligently taking time each day to enter the silence of meditation. This is an ancient discipline, one that has been practiced by the masters from time immemorial. It is the "road less traveled" by the masses, but it is the road that leads to light, wisdom, peace, knowledge, and, most importantly, communion with the Most High.

From the heights of the realms of the Great White Brotherhood, here is the message that was given to the young boy, Patmore, and us. The spiritual truths of the Lama's words are as universally applicable today as they were when they were given in the late 1800s:

[The Lama]: I greet you, my brothers, who know me not in the flesh, yet know me in the spirit. Today it shall be my joy and privilege to recall to your memories those three real truths which ye have learned in the past but have not brought over into your present rebirths . . . Know my brothers: There is but one LIFE manifesting through all forms. There is but one SELF manifesting through all selves. There is but one LOVE manifesting through all loves. The SELF is one with LIFE and the SELF is one with LOVE, therefore are the three but one. He who realizes his unity with the LIFE, SELF and LOVE knoweth Bliss, for pure LIFE is Bliss, the pure SELF is Bliss, and pure (unconditional) LOVE is Bliss. When the sun shines through crimson glass there appears to be a crimson sun, and when the sun shines through emerald glass there appears to be an emerald sun, yet there is but one sun which is neither crimson nor emerald. And so it is with the one SELF shining through a myriad [of] individual selves, which are as but the coloured windows through which the sun of SELF doth shine. These truths which I have enunciated are the great Simples, yet they are eternal profundities. Ponder on them . . . My brothers, perceive the one SELF in all beings, then will ye love all beings. In your scriptures it is written "Love thy neighbor as thyself," and ye have deemed that to mean, love thy neighbor as much as thyself. But ye err, for it also means thou shouldst love thy neighbor as thyself because he is one with thyself, seeing there is but one SELF.[12]

The essence of the Lama's message correlates with modern-day near-death experience research into the life review. As stated previously, the life review is where each soul *sees through the eyes and feels through the heart of every person they helped or hurt.* In the life review, we are our neighbor. In that light, there is no question where we have advanced in soul development and unconditional love and where we have fallen short. The Lama continued:

> Verily there are many waves in the sea, yet are those waves one with the sea . . . and their difference is not of kind but only of name and form. And so it is with thyself and thy neighbors. Only when Mankind shall realise this will all enmities cease . . . The mother of conflict is the illusion of diversity; the mother of unhappiness is the search without for that which is within. Every soul . . . is striving to find the bliss of SELF; the sage tries . . . through wisdom and saintliness and the sinner through folly and sinfulness; the desire is the same but the methods are diverse. Blame not the sinner, my brothers, but have compassion on him, for his sinfulness is but ignorance, incurring none the less its retribution, be it in the present or the future. This is . . . the law of karma, but you of the West have erased its truth from your religion, deeming that a man can evade the consequences of his misdeeds through repentance . . . Yet is the law of karma a benignant law, for if man could elude the consequences of searching for the SELF in the wrong way, how would he ever come to think to search for it in the right way? Through the ways of error doth man ultimately arrive at Truth—the Truth of the SELF which shall set him free. Peace be with you.[13]

The beauty of this message is that every human being is spiritually evolving, whether moving obviously forward or seemingly backward. The mistakes of today may create suffering tomorrow, but out of that suffering will come enlightenment. When a soul finds itself in the heart of darkness, as Howard Storm did in his near-death experience, for example, it is as the Lama says, "Through the ways of error doth man ultimately arrive at Truth . . . " Storm found himself surrounded in darkness, called out for light, and it was there for him. Had Storm not led a life of darkness, he would not be a channel of light today.

Edgar Cayce said that leading a spiritual life is not easy; in doing so, we will have to face darkness, enemies, and problems. It's easy to love one's friends; as Cayce said the real work comes in when we're face-to-face with someone who has manipulated or despitefully used us or has hurt us, seemingly without reason. What are we going to do about *them*? If we respond to them in kind, we become part of the darkness. That's where spiritual work is truly *work*. Our enemies are the ones who need our prayers the most. Like begets like. Chaos and discord breed comparable thought forms and *bring very real forces into the earth*, or each soul can be a powerful emissary for light, love, and peace. Remember "the reservoir" that the brotherhood draws from to help humanity, as spoken of by Leadbeater. When we pray for our adversaries, those prayers send light that banishes the darkness.

Forgiveness is another vital part of the spiritual path. St. Francis of Assisi said, "Hate the sin, but love the sinner." We will be forgiven only when we forgive our adversaries, our enemies. To the degree that we pass judgment, that judgment will be passed to us in equal (or larger) measure. This is the law of karma of which the Lama spoke.

Remember, everyone with whom we interact only brings us face to face with ourselves. We can recognize and feel in others only that which we have within our own selves, whether in small or large part. The goodness and inspiration we recognize in a spiritual teacher or master resonates with our own inner goodness and inspiration. The same is true of the weakness and darkness we see in others. We are all in the process of becoming masters. As we open ourselves as channels of help and hope to others, our spiritual growth is accelerated, and, step by step, we will be led to the next level of our spiritual evolution. We are, as Jesus said, "gods" in the making.

When we turn our attention within and ask, in reverence and humility, be directed by the Most High, we are not *beneath* the masters and the Great White Brotherhood. *They are the image of our future; we are a reflection of them in the past.* The caterpillar eventually becomes the butterfly.

We might think of the brotherhood as butterflies and ourselves as the caterpillar. The winged beauty of the butterfly is already patterned within the caterpillar as it grows and changes from the caterpillar to the chrysalis. It is only a matter of time and patience before we one day fly free. Then, moving on to a higher state of consciousness, we will be another step closer to conscious communion with the Creator. Our only requirement is to try to be a channel of unconditional love. We are aligned with the brotherhood when we try to emulate them and follow the pattern of the Master of Masters—to love one another as He loves us—unconditionally, eternally. It is a process of growth, and, as we consciously look to God for inspiration and direction, the Creator sends angels, guides and the elders to nurture and guide us to the next step, carrying us closer to that eternal light of unconditional love.

6

Questions and Answers on Death, Dying, and the Afterlife

These are approached, then, from the phase of the entity's soul development. For many are those awarenesses that must be sought for, if the entity would bring into this experience that which will make for the peace and harmony that comes only with the consideration of life as a whole.

For, as has been given, it is not all of life to live, nor yet all of death to die. For life and death are one, and only those who will consider the experience as one may come to understand or comprehend what peace indeed means.

Edgar Cayce reading 1977-1

Since the publication of my last book, *The Place We Call Home*, in 2000, I have traveled extensively, presenting programs, seminars, and retreats based on the Edgar Cayce readings and other sources on the afterlife, near-death experiences, and after-death communications. During the seminars, I speak on the soul's journey through the death transition, both from sudden circumstances and under gradual conditions, such as a terminal illness. I emphasize the importance of prayer and meditation after a loved one dies, for they still need our help in the early stages after death, and the power of prayer cannot be underestimated. Edgar Cayce said that, "Those who have passed on need the prayers of those have live aright." (3416-1) The bond of love we share with a loved one still exists after death; the *relationship* remains. All that has happened is that they have moved on to a new locale and left the body behind.

On this vast subject of the continuity of life beyond physical death,

I've drawn together some of the most frequently asked questions from my seminars. I hope these questions and answers will help illumine the spiritual path upon which we all travel, for, one day, we shall all journey through "God's Other Door" to the next stage of life. Remember, the more we learn here and now about that journey, relinquishing our fears about the death transition, the more peaceful, beautiful, and serene the transition will be.

We are in the process of creating the consciousness now that will determine the kind of experience we have in our passage into the afterlife. Many people in hospitals, especially in the West, struggle and are afraid as they near the end of their lives. Some leave this world "kicking and screaming" all the way out the door. Why? Because they have never learned—really learned—that death is only a change, a passage. Nothing is lost; consciousness survives. Now, more than ever, however, there is a wealth of information on what happens when we die, and the stages through which we will pass after the transition. Edgar Cayce's readings are always reassuring when they speak about the transition from this world to the next:

> . . . there is no death, only the transition from the physical to the spiritual plane. Then, as birth into the physical is given as the time of the new life, just so then, in physical is the birth into the spiritual life. (136-33)

The answers to the questions in this chapter are drawn from a variety of sources: my own experiences, my studies of the Cayce readings, and other spiritual source material. Quoted readings are noted by reading numbers, and other source materials are listed in the Endnotes.

Question: Do we, in our grief at the passing of loved ones, hinder their advancement on the astral plane?
Answer: The Edgar Cayce readings say that, after physical death, the soul is free from the material world, but that it is not free from matter. In other words, those who have passed still have deep

connections with the people they have loved, the places they lived, etc. They are aware of our feelings, needs, and thoughts. If we despair, it makes it difficult for them to move on to the higher realms. They may feel obligated to linger near us until we have gained sufficient self-control. A great deal of the sadness that we feel when a loved one passes is due to self-pity. Our effort should be to overcome our thought of self and to contemplate the good, the wonder, and the freedom our loved one is experiencing. The Cayce readings also say that deep prayer and meditation can help us draw closer to the "oneness" of the realms of life and death. As we pray for our departed loved one, it not only is much easier for them to move on, but also easier for us to move beyond grief into healing.

Q: What do the readings say about burial and cremation? Which is preferable?

A: Cayce said the wishes and beliefs of the deceased need to be taken into consideration in making this decision. In general, however, he said the best way to dispose of the physical body is by cremation. The question was asked, "What is the best disposition of a body, for the sake of all?" Cayce answered, "By fire!" (275-29). This viewpoint was echoed by the great Christian mystic and seer, Flower A. Newhouse.[1] She said, "Cremation is preferable to burial because it immediately frees the higher bodies from the physical and etheric shroud. Until an etheric body is dissolved, the higher vehicles are unable to permanently leave the vicinity of the body. It is better to give an individual immediate freedom through cremation."[2]

Q: Do our friends who have experienced death know of our present lives?

A: Yes. Keep in mind, the only thing that has changed at death is the shedding of the body. Those who precede us in death have an intuitive sense that keeps them informed about our activities and progress. Edgar Cayce said that, in some cases, souls who pass on will remain in and around the family, helping them to overcome their grief. In a sense, our deceased loved ones can act in the capacity of guardian angels for a period of time after death, staying near us until we get over the initial shock and grief. Eventually, however, our loved ones on the other side must turn their attention to their new environment, where their learning, growth, and expansion of consciousness carry them onward, away from the earth. The bond of love we have shared with them still exists, but they have lessons to learn and schools to attend, in order to further their own spiritual development.

It seems that our deceased loved ones are closest to us immediately after death, and for some varying time afterward. It is very important for us to not "hold them back" by longing for their companionship or through condemning the circumstances of their death. This is selfishness. One day, we will meet those we love again—and it will be a joyous reunion. In the relationship with those who have passed on, real love is letting go and helping them move more easily into the Higher Realms. If we do not do this, we can hinder their progress, and that will, in turn, retard our own spiritual development.

Q: Do you believe prayer helps the departed and, if so, how?

A: Yes. Flower Newhouse said that prayer creates a vibration or light that travels to the one for whom it is intended. In the dimensions known as the astral world, which the soul inhabits immediately after death, thoughts are seen and felt—they take on form. When we pray for those we love who are in these realms, our prayers not only are observable by them, but also they are strong messengers of energy and encouragement. The prayers for the dead are literally forces of light that help direct the departed to move higher, to the realms of the Light. A sincere prayer for our loved one might appear before them as a beautiful angel or light-being, and our loved one does, indeed, know from whom the prayer comes.

In an earlier chapter I discussed *The Boy Who Saw True*, the diary of a psychically gifted child who could see and communicate with the dead. The ten-year-old boy wrote the following endearing passage about the conversation he had had with his deceased grandfather, about prayers for those who have passed on:

> We [the boy and his tutor, Mr. Patmore] had just been having history about the Protestants breaking off from the cathlics [sic] and the cathlics [sic] saying mass for the dead and all that, and we were wondering what grandpa and the spirits thought about it. Then all at once I saw old grandpa, and he said the Protestants did quite wrong not to pray for people when they are what we call dead, because unselfish prayers are beautiful thoughts that make a lovely light round the spirits and help them a lot and let them know we are thinking of them too, which gives them pleasure and reminds them they are not forgotten.[3]

Also, Edgar Cayce said that many souls who have "erred" during their earthly lives, have been "saved" by the prayers of those still on earth! In short, we can, through prayer, help them become free from earthbound thoughts and desires. In one of the most beautiful passages I know in the Cayce readings, he said:

> Yea, pray oft for those who have passed on . . . those who have passed through God's other door are oft listening, listening for the voice of those they have loved in the earth.
> . . . thy prayers direct [the loved one] closer to that throne of love and mercy, that pool of light, yea, that river of God. 3954-1

Q: Did Edgar Cayce give a specific prayer to aid those who have passed on?

A: Yes. It was given in one of the series of readings for the Glad Helpers prayer group, in response to the request, "Please give a prayer for those who have passed on." Cayce responded, "Father, in Thy love, Thy mercy, be Thou near those who are in—and have recently entered—the Borderland. May I aid, when Thou seest that Thou canst use me." (281-15) I say this prayer at nighttime, before going to sleep. Cayce said that sleep is a shadow of that we call death and that every soul leaves the body during sleep. I intuitively feel the urge to say this prayer before sleep so that I might be used to help those in need on the other side. In sleep, we are in the realms of the deceased. In both our daily waking lives and during sleep, we can be a channel of help, hope, and light to others. It's also important to remember to say the names of the departed for whom you are praying. When I use this prayer, I say, "Father, in Thy love, in Thy mercy, be Thou near [here I list the names of people on my "passed on" list] who are in—and have recently entered the Borderland," etc. The vibration of the name resonates with the soul who has passed on. I picture the person for whom I am praying, surrounded in light, love, and serenity.

Q: Does the soul enter the child at conception, or birth, or in between?

A: In answer to this question, Edgar Cayce said, "It [the soul] may [enter] at the first moment of breath; it may some hours before birth; it may many hours after birth." (457-10) This might seem like a strange answer. If the soul sometimes doesn't enter the body until many hours after birth, what keeps the body alive? The same mechanism that keeps the body alive when we sleep. Although we are out of the body during sleep, there is a primary spiritual force that enables us to breathe, the heart to beat, and all involuntary functions of the autonomic nervous system to continue. This, according to the readings is "the God-Force." Neither science nor medicine really knows how these functions continue automatically, even while we sleep or are otherwise unconscious. Cayce said it is because of the working of the spirit, through the body, from the spiritual Source.

This connection between the body and spirit is unseen, but clairvoyants and seers have termed this connection "the silver cord." At physical death, that cord is severed. In sleep, however, the soul can be absent

from the body, and, because of this spiritual connection, all bodily functions continue while the soul travels in the realms of spirit.

A woman asked this very question in reading 2390-2: "What keeps
the physical body living until the soul enters?" Cayce replied, "Spirit!
For, the spirit of matter—its source is life, or God . . . "

Cayce gave another fascinating reading that notes the difference between the physical birth and the soul birth: " . . . in entering the present
experience [being born], we find coming in the early afternoon . . . while
the *spiritual* entrance was in the late evening." (1397-1) This certainly
throws a wrench into astrological birth profile charts, for the soul can
enter later on after birth!

**Q: Why do some souls enter into the earth plane for
only a few days, months, or years?**

A: Edgar Cayce gave different reasons why souls come in for
only short periods. In one reading Edgar Cayce said, "Many souls
are seeking to enter, but not all are attracted. Some may be repelled. Some are attracted and then suddenly repelled, so that the
life in the earth is only a few days." (281-53)

In another reading, he said that, when a soul incarnates on the earth
for only a short period of time, the experience has a vast impact upon
the soul:

> "Hence the reincarnation into this or that influence, and those
> [souls] that are only aware of [the] material [world] or carnal
> influences for a moment may be as greatly impressed as were a finite
> mind for a moment in the presence of Infinity. When one considers
> the birth of a soul into the earth, the more often is the body and the
> body-mind considered than the soul—that [the soul] is full-grown
> in a breath . . . (262-57)

We might use the example of the near–death experience to illustrate what Cayce is saying here. Some NDE's last only a few seconds, and yet, the impact upon the soul in terms of expansion of consciousness is so profound that it affects the individual for the rest of that life. Cayce was saying that the same is true for a soul who comes to earth for a few moments or days: That experience can have equally as transforming an effect upon the soul and its development as a near–death experience does for someone who returns to life.

Flower Newhouse was asked by a bereaved mother why her ten-year-old child was taken from this life so abruptly, though quietly and without pain. I have shared Newhouse's inspiring answer with many bereaved parents, who find peace and solace in spite of their sorrow:

When a child who is spiritually and mentally developed finishes certain earth experiences, she is sometimes allowed release from the earth in an easy and sudden manner. The immediate and surprising transition of your lovely daughter would make me feel that she was an advanced soul who came into your family to bring a blessing to it, and to finish some lesson or obligation she owed to earth experience. That she was able to graduate from this training school of life so young and in a manner comparatively easy as she did, reveals her spiritual development. It will be your task to realize that she was God's child and only lent to you for ten blessed years . . . [and] for you to appreciate that you had her ten years rather than ten days. The inner reasons for God's advancing this soul who came into your family may never be fully known to you . . . Think only of the blessings which she brought to you and be *grateful* for them.

When children go out as this one did, they are taken into a realm of great beauty where Angelic Ones, called *Watcher Beings,* are like governesses to hosts of young children. They are kept on a level which agrees with their stage of spiritual advancement. For instance, your daughter will progress from that Happy Region, as it is called, more quickly than others; but you can visualize her as being in a very blessed, peaceful, and scenic area for several years. During her stay in this region, she will be very conscious of all the thoughts of her parents and family. You must do your utmost to overcome grief by *trusting* in God's will and by trying to release the whole experience into the love and care of the Father. Someday you will know why this advanced soul came to you, and you will understand what great treasure you received through her coming . . . ⁴

Edgar Cayce also told some parents that souls may come to earth for brief periods for the spiritual awakening of the parents. It may be that their spiritual awakening could occur only after a great deal of grief and pain and sense of loss. In order to deal with such sorrow, parents often begin to search for a deeper spiritual meaning to life and death. Eventually, they may come across spiritual material such as the Cayce readings or other spiritual information that affirms that there truly is no death, that it is only the "the passing through God's Other Door." In the dark night of the soul, we search for the light. I have seen parents who lost a child—and there is no darker night of the soul than this experience—and these people, indeed, had a spiritual awakening. Because of their experience, they then can help other parents whose children have died. Many become bereavement counselors or speak or write on the subject. They come to believe that we never truly lose those we love.

So, the reasons for a child entering this world and departing early are multifaceted. In all the Cayce readings I've seen, I am not aware of a single case where he placed blame for the circumstances of a child dying young on something the parents did or neglected to do. In many cases, he said that the soul had changed its mind—that the opportunities weren't right for the soul to incarnate at that particular time, and the soul had "chosen to remain with its Maker."

Q: I recently lost my husband and feel so alone without him. Why does it seem that we often lose our loved ones at a time when we need them the most?

A: The earth is a school, a place of learning, and the realms of the afterlife are our true home. When a soul leaves this earthly school, it has earned a period of rest and release from material concerns, pressures, and struggles. Those of us left behind also need to gain or regain independence and self–reliance. Pray often for your husband, and give thanks to God for all the time He gave for you to be together. Realize, too, that there is no such thing as a *permanent* farewell; those whom we love, we will meet again. Love is a bond that can be broken by neither time nor space.

Edgar Cayce advised that we turn our attention within, in meditation, to seek the comfort and solace that is beyond words. Ask in prayer, before meditation, to experience "the peace and serenity of God that passeth worldly understanding." Desire to experience that with all your heart and soul. Continue this practice daily. After a time, you *will* experience the peace, the comfort, the reassurance that no one we have loved is ever lost. Our trek through this material world is but a moment in eternity. You will be reunited with those whom you love, after you pass from this life. As author Richard Bach said, "Don't be dismayed at good–byes. A farewell is necessary before we can meet again, and meeting again, after moments or lifetimes, is certain for those who are friends."[5]

Q: I seem to recall that Edgar Cayce said the earth is "shadow" or a "reflection" of the spiritual world. Did he say that, and what exactly does that mean?

A: Yes, Cayce said that many times in the readings. The best way I can explain that is that the material world is only a pale reflection of what exists in the *real* world–which is the world of spirit. I've talked to people who had near–death experiences, and after they returned, they tried, with a great deal of frustration, to describe the indescribable colors they saw while they were "dead." They talk about flowers, trees, and birds that are so breathtakingly beautiful, it makes what we have on earth a mere caricature. Everything that is manifest in material form has its source in the spiritual dimensions. Cayce often said, "Spirit is the Life, Mind is the Builder, the Physical is the result." What we see on earth is the finite representation of a spiritual reality. People who return from NDEs talk about hearing "living music"—or what Cayce called "the music of the spheres." If you've ever heard a beautiful piece of music that moved you to the heights of great emotion, just imagine how that music must sound in the spiritual world!

The earth is a mirror of the spiritual dimensions. In *The Boy Who Saw True*, the psychic child asked his deceased grandfather how the physical world looked to him. The grandfather said everything looks rather shadowy, and human beings (in body) look like ghosts! He said that souls who are free from physical form can easily walk through solid material objects such doors, walls, etc., because the atoms and molecules of so-called solid objects are, in fact, spaced so far apart that souls can walk right through them, just as we walk through fog in the material world. So our material world is literally a realm of vague shadows of what exists in the real world of spirit.

We might think of it in terms of dimensions. In sunlight, three-dimensional objects cast two-dimensional shadows. Carry that a step further and think about this: Fourth-dimensional realities (spirit) cast three-dimensional "shadows" (the world of materiality). In this light, it's understandable why so many people return from their NDEs so surprised by what they saw. They learned that there's no difference between the here and the hereafter, except that the spiritual realities are far more real than anything we ever experience on earth. Is it any wonder that few people who have glimpsed the afterlife in an NDE do not want to return to earth? If the earth contains the shadows or reflections of the arts we cherish—great symphonies, ballets, paintings, and literature—imagine what the spiritual originals from which those arts emanate must be like in the spirit world. It must be Heaven.

Q: Do the readings have anything to say about the relationship of senility to the transition of dying, and does the soul leave the body prior to physical death?

A: Yes, there are numerous readings that say something such as, "Yes, we have the entity, not the body—the entity just waits by here until the final separations are made." The "final separation" is when the soul leaves the body for good. When someone is terminally ill and nearing death, we often describe them as being "in and out" of consciousness. What we are really saying is that the soul is in and out of the body. At a lecture program, Hugh Lynn Cayce commented on this subject:

When a person is very, very sick, the soul has already gotten out of the body and is just standing by waiting for the functions of the flesh body to cease, that it withdraws well ahead of time . . . Frequently where the brain has deteriorated or where there is illness over a long period of time, the soul is moving in and out all the time and has already stepped out, while the flesh is just continuing on through the physical functioning . . . [6]

Q: When my mother was dying from cancer, the whole family was on a twenty-four-hour watch by her bedside. During the brief period when we all stepped out of the room to get a cup of coffee, Mother died. We couldn't have been out of the room longer than ten minutes. What does such an experience mean? I've felt badly that no one was there with her.

A: This happens more frequently than you might imagine. Let me reassure you that, if you were supposed to be there when she made her transition, you would have been. Often, the soul seems to need this final transition from this world to the next to be a very private affair.

Additionally, when a family is gathered around the bedside of a someone who is dying, there are very few of us, in the West at least, who can bring ourselves to encourage the soul to let go and go to the light. Most family members are grieving and hoping for some miracle to happen so the dying person can recover. Under such circumstances, it can be very difficult for the soul to finally and completely let go of the physical and move on.

At some level, the transitioning soul is aware of the thoughts and emotions of those in the room. This is not to say that families are consciously holding the soul back. Remember that, in the final stages, the soul may be partly or completely out of the body. But it's somewhat like being at a family reunion that you're trying to leave and everybody is saying, "Oh, don't go! Stay a little longer, please!" How easy is it for you to leave when people you love are begging you to stay? Not very. In some cases, you have to slip out the back door to get away from the people who are saying, "Don't leave yet!" When your family all stepped out of the room for coffee, it was the easiest time for your mother to finally let go of the body. Rest assured that all the love you showed your mother while at her bedside was enough so that, when everyone stepped out of the room, she felt free to go.

We've been taught, erroneously, that we are supposed to be there when a person dies. Realize that, in the final stages before the soul takes leave of this earthly realm, it is in the companionship of guides and guardian angels and has been moving in and out of the spirit realms throughout the transition. When the "final step" is made at death, the soul is on familiar ground and in good hands. Do not berate yourself that you weren't present when she finally left. She didn't need you to be there at that final moment. In all the years I have been involved with hospice, I've never been present when one of the patients to whom I was assigned made their transition. Not once.

Q: How can we make the death transition easier for a terminally ill patient?

A: I remember a reading Edgar Cayce gave for a child who was terminally ill. He said that the child needed nothing except reassurance about the "beauties of the transition." As you sit by the bedside of a dying person, be very aware of your thoughts and your words. Whenever possible, hold their hand, and tell them that all is well, that a beautiful light is present and that there are angels all around them. Give them permission to leave; that is very important. Many are waiting to hear that from their loved ones. I realize that some families are not open to these things, so if you can't say them aloud, then direct your thoughts in this direction to the dying patient. Remember that, although they may be in a coma, their soul–mind is very aware of words spoken in their presence and the thoughts of people in the room. The more we can send them light—in prayer, in thought, and in the spoken word—the easier the transition can be. There is a wonderful book that I highly recommend, entitled *The Tibetan Book of Living and Dying* by Sogyal Rinpoche. This book has prayers and meditations for those who are in transition, as well as prayers for those who have passed on. These prayers are extremely helpful to the soul in transition, and their experience of death can be one of great peace and serenity.

Q: What happens when a soul commits suicide?

A: First of all, it's tempting to want to look for a single answer to some of life's most troubling questions, including the subject of suicide. Dr. Raymond Moody researched NDEs in attempted suicides, and what he learned is worth mentioning here:

> All of these people [who attempted suicide] agree on one point: they felt their suicidal attempts solved nothing. They found that they were involved in exactly the same problems [on the Other Side] from which they had been trying to extricate themselves by suicide. Whatever difficulty they had been trying to get away from was still there on the other side, unresolved . . . One person mentioned being "trapped" in the situation which had provoked her suicide attempt. She had the feeling that the state of affairs in which she had been in before her "death" was being repeated again and again, as if in a cycle . . . All [the people who had NDEs during a suicide attempt] mentioned that after their experiences, they would never consider trying suicide again. Their common attitude is that they had made a mistake, and that they were very glad they had not succeeded . . . I asked one man whether, in the light of what he had experienced, he would ever again choose to try to kill himself, he answered: "No. I would not do that again . . . because one thing I realized at that time is that our life here is just such a small period of time and there is so much which needs to be done while you're here. And, when you die it's eternity."[7]

Dr. George Ritchie, the author who detailed his nine-minute NDE in his book, *Return from Tomorrow*[8], was shown, during his death experience, the realm where souls go who commit "vengeful suicides." These, according to Dr. Ritchie, are the cases where people chose to kill themselves in order to make someone still living feel guilty about their death. Dr. Ritchie saw, in the after-death state, that these souls were bound to the very people they tried to hurt by their suicide. They were "trapped in time," so to speak, so that they were constantly in the presence of the person they spitefully tried to hurt. It was a pathetic sight. It was if the hurt they tried to inflict on another rebounded to take possession of their soul instead, and its effect was magnified to the point that the person was literally in a hellish state of being. According to Dr. Ritchie, these souls are released from this hellish realm only after they take full responsibility for their selfish and vengeful act, ask for forgiveness, and ask for help from God. Until they reach that point, they are caught in the web of their own making.

Dr. Ritchie is very careful, however, to say that there is an exception to this situation: those who commit suicide because of mental illness. They may be schizophrenic, experiencing horrifying hallucinations; in these cases, the individual kills themselves to stop the terrifying visions. They may suffer from such severe depression that they lose all hope. He believes that these souls are cared for by the higher beings on the other side. In these cases, the suicide is not a result of selfishness, but of a desperate attempt to free oneself from the terrifying effects of their illness. Prayer for those who have committed suicide (or for those on the other side who have no one to pray for them) should not be underestimated. It provides a great deal of help to the soul, and the prayers eventually will help many of those find their way to the light.

Q: How can we break the cycle of "the wheel of reincarnation?" In other words, what must we do to be free from having to return for another "go-around?"

A: A unique and very insightful answer to this question was transcribed by the psychic child in *The Boy Who Saw True*. He was communicating with one of the elders of the Great White Brotherhood, and, at the prompting of Mr. Patmore, his teacher, he asked:

"Do . . . we have to go on dying and being reborn at given periods for the rest of all time?"

"No," the elder said. "Only till you have ceased to generate causes on the physical plane which must have their effects on the physical plane. To give you a trite example. The ordinary man on earth usually saddles himself with business ties, social ties, family ties, and a thousand duties and responsibilities which he can't get out of, and which tie him to a given place. He may take a yearly holiday, but sooner or later he has to return to resume his business activities, pay and collect his debts, and fulfill all his other obligations. Having in the first place created all those responsibilities, he has to go through with them whether he likes it or not. It is the same with the soul, only in a much vaster sense. The soul has created ties and obligations on earth through its desire to make money, have a family, acquire possessions, social standing and many other 'treasures on earth.' All these are ties which eventually bring it [the soul] back to the earth-plane, to teach it wisdom through experience. If it has sown evil, it comes back to reap the effects of that evil and adjust its debts through suffering. If it has sown good, it comes back to reap the effects of that good. If it has sown a mixture of both good and evil, as most of us have, it comes back to reap the effects of both good and evil, in which case its incarnation will be a medley of so-called good luck and bad. [In order to not be required to come to earth anymore], the soul has to lay up for itself treasures in heaven instead of treasures on earth. First of all he must avoid doing evil so as to incur no debts to be paid off in a future incarnation, and secondly, he must do good for its own sake without any desire for reward. Because strong desires, unless unselfish, have sooner or later to be fulfilled, they are fetters which bind one to earth. Strong desires act somewhat like a boomerang; you hurl them forth in time in the shape of desires, and they come back to you in the shape of fulfillments. Say, in a given incarnation a man strongly wishes for some sort of fame, but circumstances are against him and he dies before his wish has been gratified. What happens? Through his powerful wish, he has generated subtle forces which cannot just disappear into nothing-ness any more than a boomerang can just disappear into space, so he has eventually to come back to experience the gratification of his wish . . . Most people want to be wealthy, to wield power, to occupy high positions, or to shine in society. All these desires, which are actuated by vanity, are the lassoes which catch the soul and drag it back into incarnation."[9]

It's important to understand from the elder's words here that wealth, power, and high positions, in themselves, are not evil; it is our attachment to them that makes them evil. It's been said that, "Money is the root of all evil." The elder said the same thing but used a different word: He said *attachment* to evil is the root of all evil. In order to live freely and happily and not be "earth bound," we must not allow ourselves to be dependent on external things for happiness. "For the only true and lasting happiness is to be found within," the elder said.[10] So the more unattached we can become in this life, relinquishing the attachments to things, to habits, to patterns of behavior that are at variance to spiritual harmony, then, as the Master put it, " . . . the truth shall make you free." (John 8:32)

7

Chronicles of the Afterlife

For in that sleep of death what dreams may come,
When we have shuffled off this mortal coil,
Must give us pause.

Hamlet, Act III, Scene 1

In 1998 and 1999, Hollywood released two dramatic films abou various dimensions of the afterlife: *What Dreams May Come* a *Sixth Sense.*

In *The Sixth Sense*, a little boy was psychically attuned to pe had died. "I see dead people," the boy said to a psychiatri y Bruce Willis. "But they don't know they're dead." The h oy Haley Joel Osment, was terrified by his clairvoyant vi the help of the psychiatrist, the boy realized that some of t ople" were showing up because they needed his help. One fright- ening of his visions was a woman who had slashed her wrists. She stood, bleeding, in the kitchen, yelling and complaining (as she obviously had done when she was alive) at a husband who was no longer there but who was the real object of the hurt she wished to inflict. In such cases of "selfish" suicides, the soul does not depart the earth, nor is it free of the troubling circumstances that led to the suicide.

One of the recently deceased souls the boy saw was a little girl who came for his help. Her mother had murdered her by gradually poisoning her food. The girl had been sick for a very long time, and her death mystified her father and her doctors. The boy went to the girl's home after her funeral, and she showed him where she had hidden a video tape that she secretly had made of her mother putting poison in her food. The boy took the tape to the girl's father and said, "She wanted you to have this." As he left the house, the father inserted the tape and watched, horrified, amid his guests, as the mother brought in her daughter's lunch tray and then put poison into the soup. All eyes turned to the mother. "You made her sick," the father said, weeping. "You did it."

Just as in this movie, in real life, the souls of those who were murdered or died under mysterious circumstances sometimes will not rest or move on until the truth about their death is told. Detectives, in particular, are sought out by these souls because such investigators often pay close attention to their intuition or "hunches," hunches that may be prompted by contact with their subconscious by the restless souls. Synchronistic events that solve a murder often are prompted by souls on the other side as they attempt to communicate through friends, loved ones, the police, or psychic sensitives.

The director of *The Sixth Sense* grew up in India, in a family he has described as having a deep understanding of the afterlife. From the time he was a little boy, he knew that some souls remain around their earthly environs for varying lengths of time. Often, it is some unfinished business that leads the soul to remain on earth, to provide information about their death or, perhaps, to help with a matter that they had the opportunity to help during their earthly lives, but did not. Many people think that, when physical death comes, the opportunities for growth end or the soul must "start over." Nothing could be further from the truth. In *The Sixth Sense*, moviegoers saw how the soul simply changes form—and dimensions—at physical death, but the opportunity for growth and development carries on. One character in the film, for example, died unexpectedly but didn't realize that he was dead. He went about his daily life just as he had before he died. Once he completed the selfless task of helping the boy, he realized that he had died, and then he could move on. Edgar Cayce said that Heaven is not a place to which we go, it is a realm to which we grow, on the arm of someone we have helped. Just so, the character fulfilled his soul's obligations and then was able to pass on to a higher realm.

Another film, *What Dreams May Come*, delved even more deeply into the afterlife. Based on the 1978 novel by Richard Matheson, this dramatic story holds a great deal of truth about the many dimensions of the afterlife. Although it is fiction, it was based on the experiences of someone to whom the author was very close.

"Because [this book's] subject is survival after death," Matheson wrote, "it is essential that you realize, before reading the story, that only one aspect of it is fictional: The characters and their relationships. _With few exceptions, every other detail is derived exclusively from research._" [author's emphasis][1]

At the end of the book, Matheson listed the books that inspired him to write _What Dreams May Come;_ I have included several of those books in the Bibliography and Suggested Reading List at the end of this book. Though some of these titles are out of print, it is worth the effort to locate them. After my extensive reading of many of these classic texts on the spiritual worlds that await us after physical death, I wholeheartedly agree with Matheson, who wrote:

> . . . the books used for this research . . . they are many and diverse. Yet, despite their wide variation with regard to authors and times and places of publication, there is a persistent, unavoidable uniformity to their content. You would, of course, have to read them all to prove this to yourself. I urge you to do so. You will find it an enlightening—and extraordinary experience.[2]

The striking correlation of the descriptions of the after-death dimensions among these books is nothing short of extraordinary. Whether the information came from near-death experiencers or from psychics and channelers, there is an across-the-board tone of urgency coming from the other side that we need to wake up, take stock of ourselves, look beyond the world of earthly things that hold most of us hypnotically spellbound, and ask ourselves, "Where would I go if I died tomorrow? What do I know of my soul and my relationship to God? How do I respond to and treat the people around me, day by day?" The answers to these questions have everything to do with where we will find ourselves after death. So many souls cross over the threshold of physical death, completely unprepared for what awaits them. The good news is that the majority of souls, though they may have confined themselves to narrow beliefs about the afterlife, will be happily surprised to awaken in a realm that is more expansive and more enjoyable than they ever dreamed.

Richard Matheson's protagonist, Chris Nielson, eventually found himself in a quite enjoyable place after death, though he had to pass through some difficult experiences prior to arriving there, due to his own stubbornness. When he died, he was in the prime of his life and deeply in love with his wife, Ann. A head-on car collision brought his physical life to a grinding, crashing halt. Much like Dr. George Ritchie, the character was "between the worlds" when he was taken to the emergency room. He could hear his wife crying, and he felt her suffering for him. He desperately tried to hold on to physical life in his body, but he felt himself leaving his body anyway. Though his heart's desire was to be with his wife, a reassuring voice from an unseen being told him to just relax and let go. Chris fought against that voice—he couldn't imagine life without Ann, the light of his life. Then, he found himself experiencing the life review of every event of his life—from the last day he lived on earth, back to his own birth. Finally, he slipped into what felt like sleep but actually was the final stage of his death.

When Chris woke up in a hospital room, he felt better and more alive than he ever had. The memories of the car accident and of his wife crying had grown vague; he thought it was all a dream. Then, a nurse and a doctor came rushing into the room. He spoke to them and couldn't figure out why they ignored him. He tried to grab the doctor's coat, and his hand swept right through it. Chris thought he must be in surgery, under anesthesia, and that all this was a dream.

Many aspects of Chris's fictional experience were quite similar to the near-death experience of Dr. George Ritchie. In the first few minutes after he died, Dr. Ritchie didn't realize he was dead. He kept trying to get the attention of the people in the hospital hallway. Everyone ignored him. Infuriated by such blatant disregard, Dr. Ritchie decided to stand his ground and block one man's path. "He'll have to run over me," he thought. "I'm not moving until he answers me." It appeared as though

In Matheson's novel, Chris' first reunion was with his big, friendly dog, Katie. She came bounding over to Chris with loving enthusiasm. He was overcome with joy at seeing the dog he had loved so dearly on earth for sixteen years. In the Summerland, she was once again in the prime of her life. According to those who have been to the other side, our beloved animals also have a consciousness that is part of the Divine Spirit and that continues after their physical death, even though they do not have the free will that human beings do. All forms of life—which is energy—are indestructible and eternal; everything that lives on earth will live on in the spirit world.

In *The Boy Who Saw True*, as the young clairvoyant sat with his beloved tutor and the tutor's wife, Mr. and Mrs. Patmore, he saw the spiritual form of a large, black Labrador retriever, curled up near the couple's feet. The boy asked them if they had ever had a dog. The two looked at one another and were very sad. They answered that they had had a dog for many years, who was a light in both of their lives, but that she had passed away. The boy wrote in his diary that, at the mention of the dog's name, the Lab happily wagged its tail and sat up, looking at the Patmores. The boy accurately described their beloved dog and said he was right there with them still. They were overjoyed.

There have been many stories of people who, after their pets died, heard claws clicking on the floors or on the hallway steps. Nor is it uncommon for people to wake up in the night and feel the warmth and weight of their once-beloved pet, sleeping at their feet. When they come to full waking, however, the feeling passes; the "phantom glimpsing" of pets is just their way of telling us that they continue to love us and be with us. Likewise, pets can and will be with us after death, in the realms of the Summerland, just as Matheson wrote in *What Dreams May Come*.

Next, Chris had a reunion with his beloved cousin, Albert, who arrived in a flash of light. Albert said he had been near Chris for the last twenty years, acting as Chris's guardian angel or spirit guide. This parallels the Cayce readings that say that no one travels through the earthly experience alone but is always in the companionship of guardian angels, who sometimes may be our deceased friends or family members. The term *angel* means *messenger*. It is an office that many souls volunteer to carry out for their remaining loved ones on earth. They work from the realms of the Summerland to help us, to lend inspiration, and to console us.

It was Albert who had encouraged Chris to let go, just before he died. He was also present when Chris was in the "gray world" between the earth and the higher worlds:

> "Why didn't I recognize you after I died?" Chris asked. "It was you in the hospital who told me not to fight it, wasn't it?
>
> "I was trying to break through," Albert said. "Make your transition less painful . . . There was no way of getting to you. You were so intent on reaching your wife . . . It was very loving of you but it trapped you in the borderland."
>
> "That was horrible," Chris said.
>
> "It could have been far worse though. You might have lingered there for months or years—centuries even. It's not uncommon. If you hadn't called for help—"
>
> "You mean, until I called for help, there was nothing that you could do?"
>
> "I tried but you kept rejecting me . . . It was only when the vibration of your call came through that I could hope to convince you . . . "[3]

Just as in the material world, so in the afterlife: You cannot help those who do not ask for or do not want your help. Also, while many of us are very available to help others, we often have a difficult time asking for help for ourselves when we need it. It's important to remember that, if we don't ask for assistance from the people in this world, we deny them the opportunity to be of service, to be a "being of light," so to speak, and that denies them an opportunity to grow spiritually. Also, if you are stubborn and won't ask for help when you need it here on earth, then you'll be hesitant to ask for assistance on the other side, after death. Most of the time this is the result of stubborn pride—and as you can see from Chris's experience, sometimes it takes getting the wind knocked out of our sails before we can reach out and ask for help.

The Summerland is an expansive world—a place of reflection, review, and remembrance. Above all else, it is a place where what you imagine immediately comes into being. Matheson wrote:

> The very atmosphere of the Summerland is malleable. It, literally, reproduces the image of any sustained thought. It's like a mold waiting for imprints. Except for our bodies, no form is stable unless concentrated thought makes it so . . . On earth, before anything is created materially, it has to be created mentally . . . When matter is put aside, all creation becomes exclusively mental . . . the power of mind.[4]

In the physical body, we exist in the material world. In our minds, we exist in many more worlds, based upon our thoughts, feelings, and inspirations. Just so, within the sphere of the Summerland, there are many worlds within the one. As many inhabitants as live in the Summerland are how many individual worlds are there. In this, we can see echoed Edgar Cayce's assertion that the earth "is only an atom in a universe of worlds." Each individual is a universe of worlds within themselves, having physical, mental and spiritual attributes:

> For . . . each entity has within itself the possibilities of the universal consciousness. These may be obtained by the analysis of the body with its emotions, its limitations, its desires, its hopes, its fears; and by an analysis of the mind-body and of the soul-body. For as the entity finds, it is in a three-dimensional plane of experience . . . the mind is capable of exploring many dimensions . . . (3685-1)

As spiritual beings on earth, we are limited by our finite, physical existence, but the mind and spirit are not limited. In deep prayer and meditation, we can glimpse the higher worlds of the spirit. The more we access those realms, the higher our spirit will ascend toward greater awareness, after the death transition. It is in our best interests not to see ourselves as limited beings, but as capable of experiencing, as Cayce said, "a universal consciousness." We are only as limited in thought and in spirit as we believe that we are. Hugh Lynn Cayce frequently said, "If you feel out of the presence of God, make no mistake about who moved." The universal Source, or God, is as present with us as the air that we breathe; in fact, the very breath we do breathe is an essence of God. So we are never far away from "the light," although we may, at times, feel shrouded in darkness. Seeking spiritual enlightenment in this world—in the people we meet, in the jobs we hold, in the silence of our souls in meditation—is the soul's true heritage. In the afterlife, seeking the light becomes a literal activity. The more we seek it in the earthly experience, the more we will be attuned to that light in and through our own death transition and afterward.

Chris discovered that the world in which he lived was one of many worlds. The place that he found himself in the Summerland was the spiritual counterpart of the United States. It seems that souls gravitate to the wave length of their own country and people. In the spirit world, there is a vibrational equivalent to every country on earth. Chris could travel to another "country" within the Summerland, but he gravitated to Albert and to the people and places with which his soul resonated (and again, there is the echo of Cayce's concept that all things on the earth are reflections of that which exists in the spiritual worlds).

Albert also told Chris that, for each religion manifest on the earth plane, there is a corresponding Heaven. As Jesus said, "In my Father's house are many mansions." (John 14:2) When Chris inquired which religion was right, Albert answered, "All of them . . . and none. Buddhist, Hindu, Moslem, Christian, Jew—each has an afterlife experience which reflects his own beliefs. The Viking had his Valhalla, the American Indian his Happy Hunting Ground, the zealot his City of Gold. All are real. Each is a portion of the overall reality."[5]

The difference between the third and fourth dimensions is a difference only of vibration. An apt analogy is an airplane propeller. When it is at rest, the blades are like the third dimension—easily visible. When revved up to full speed, the airplane propeller seems to vanish—it is whirling so fast that the blades no longer are distinguishable by the human eye. That is like the fourth dimension. Why then, do we assume that the realms of the afterlife will be so different from earthly life? We continue to have a body, but it is functioning at a higher rate of vibration that cannot be seen in terms of three–dimensional space. Likewise, there are buildings, universities, beautiful waterfalls, and landscaped grounds in the afterlife. In the physical world, everything existent was first a thought before it became a thing. In the realms of spirit, the thought becomes the thing without the labor.

Chris asked about the beautiful landscapes and the buildings that he saw in the Summerland. Albert explained that they are designed by people who either enjoyed that kind of work on earth or who desired to do such work in the afterlife. Through cooperative effort, a group of souls creates a model image of a building in their minds.

"They correct the model as needed," Matheson wrote, "then instruct those who were builders on earth . . . and, together, all their minds in unified concentration, they cause the matrix to produce a full–scale impression of the structure. They stop before it's completed, correct to perfection, then proceed until solidification takes place."[6] What Matheson called "the matrix" is the ever–present creative spirit that exists all around souls in the Summerland—it is the creative Spark of the Creator.

Souls journey through the worlds to become cocreators with God. As a soul learns and builds, it draws upon the essential Spirit of God, regardless of what it is choosing to manifest. In the higher realms after death, the soul finds that everything is filled with the vibration of life. Even so–called inanimate objects have an inner spark, an inner "alive-ness." This aliveness is the Spirit of God that inhabits all things, seen and unseen, animate and inanimate. It is easy to see why the afterlife holds so much excitement for so many souls who are newly arrived. They discover a greater, more expansive world in which to explore whatever was their life's love on earth.

There are realms of literature, science, music, art, and medicine and the other healing arts. Under the banner of those five areas of interest are literally infinite worlds to discover and explore and in which to work. Chris was taken to a place of records, filled with books, some of which had not been published on earth yet. It might seem strange, but for every breakthrough in science, literature, or medicine, the earth is the plane of *manifestation;* the spiritual worlds are the planes *where break-throughs originate.* Entire soul groups work in tandem with the earth—always trying to help humanity evolve to the next step. The great medical discoveries and scientific findings on earth literally are "picked up" from the realms of spirit by scientists who are highly attuned to the spiritual dimensions. This answers the baffling question of how there can be simultaneous discoveries in different parts of the world without the discoverers being aware of the other. The elders of the Great White Brotherhood put the knowledge to be discovered into the collective unconscious of all humanity. Then, all within the spiritual worlds watch and wait for what was "put through" to be discovered. In very real terms, we are not left to our own devices here on earth. For every new disease that appears on earth, there are hosts of souls at work in the spirit worlds to help bring a cure into manifestation. Those who make the discoveries on earth may not admit it—or even be aware of it—but they are spiritually attuned to the fourth dimension, where all discoveries reside.

The portrait of the afterlife that Matheson painted in *What Dreams May Come* is beautiful, poignant, and accurate; even when the tale turns dark, it is accurate. Chris began to adapt to the afterlife, but a certain unease about Annie persisted, and he couldn't shake it. Then he learned that, back on earth, Annie had committed suicide with an overdose of sleeping pills. She had fallen into a depression after Chris' death, and even though she never believed in an afterlife up to the point of her suicide, she hoped there would be one so she could see Chris again. But if she hoped to find herself in some Heaven with him, she was gravely mistaken.

Matheson explained:

> To kill one's self is to violate the law because it deprives that self from working out the needs of its life. They think of suicide as a quick route to oblivion, an escape. Far from it . . . It merely alters a person from one form to another. Nothing can destroy the conditions from which escape was sought. A continuation under circumstances so much more painful . . . When she killed herself she merely discarded the denser part of her body. What remains is held magnetically by

earth—but where on earth [she] could be was impossible to discover. The corridor between the physical and astral worlds is, to all intents and purposes, endless.[7]

Chris and Ann were soul mates; this was why, in the Summerland, he kept experiencing that vague sense of unease whenever he thought of Ann. When he learned what had happened, he set out on a journey with Albert to save her. It was a perilous journey because Chris would have to lower his soul's vibrations to match the vibrations of the lower, darker realms in which Ann was caught. He ran the risk of becoming caught in the lower realms as well, and it would take every effort on his part to stay alert, to always surround himself with thoughts of the light, in order to get through the darkness.

The spirit writings of medium Anthony Borgia, transmitted by Robert Hugh Benson, a former clergyman who died in 1914, spoke of traveling through the darker realms beneath the Summerland in order to reach souls who were asking for help:

> The dark regions might almost be called the "Winterland," but for the fact that the earthly winter possesses a grandeur all its own, while there is nothing but abomination about the lower realms of the spirit world . . . I have actually penetrated deeply into those regions . . . such places exist solely by virtue of an inexorable law, the law of cause and effect, the spiritual reaping that succeeds the earthly sowing . . . to escape moral justice upon the earth plane is to find strict and unrelenting justice in the spirit world . . . We witnessed all manner of bestialities and grossness, and such barbarities and cruelties as the mind can scarcely contemplate . . . Every soul who lives in those awful places once lived upon the earth plane . . . The whole of these . . . regions exist by virtue of the same laws that govern the states of beauty and happiness.
>
> The beauty of the spirit world is the outward and visible expression of the spiritual progression of its inhabitants. When we have earned the right to possess things of beauty, they are given to

us through the power of creation. In this sense we can be said to have created them ourselves . . . Beauty of mind and deed can produce nothing but beauty, and hence we have flowers of heavenly beauty, trees and meadows, rivers and streams and seas of pure, glistening, crystal-clear water . . . and our own individual homes where we can surround ourselves with still more beauty . . . But ugliness of mind and deed can produce nothing but ugliness. The seeds of hideousness sown upon the earth-plane will inevitably lead to the reaping of a harvest of hideousness in the spirit world. These dark realms have been built up by the people of the earth-plane, even as they have been built up the realms of beauty.[8]

From this description, it is easy to imagine the heights of Heaven and the depths of Hell. Imagine crossing realms where souls exist who once lived on earth and cultivated prejudice, hatred, jealousy, envy, maliciousness, and greed. These thoughts, when held and cultivated during an earthly lifetime, propel the soul into realms in the afterlife that correspond to those same dark forces. God doesn't put anyone in Hell or in Heaven—it is of the soul's own choosing, and its creation. Nor does any soul need to *remain* in the darker regions, but it is up to the soul itself to change its mind, its thinking and to imagine light where there was once darkness.

This was Chris's task as he traversed, literally, the depths of Hell to get to Ann. He made a perilous journey down through realms that were accurately depicted in Dante's *Inferno* in order to reach her. Matheson laid out a well-defined explanation of the darker regions and Hell:

There's no one place called Hell . . . What men have called Hell is a vacuum in which undeveloped souls find themselves after death. A level of existence which they cannot rise above because they are unable to think abstractly but can only dwell on temporal matters.[9]

No one shared Ann's world with her; she was dreadfully alone. Her suicide put her in a world that was similar to the physical world but more in the way that a negative image is similar to the photograph. She lived in a dark, shadowy place that resembled the home she and Chris once shared, but that was broken down. Albert cautioned Chris that the task that lay ahead of him to reach Ann was going to be difficult because she had no memory of killing herself since she had never believed in an afterlife or the continuance of the soul. She lived in the house without electricity or water. Filth covered everything in sight. Weeds grew around the house instead of a lush green lawn. In life, Ann had despised a dirty room, and this entire house was her worst nightmare.

She didn't recognize Chris when he found her, and Albert told Chris that her state of denial and despair was so complete that she wouldn't believe anything he said to her. She didn't question how she came to be in this terrible place. Because she had no memory of killing herself, she thought only Chris was dead. The rest of her mind was preoccupied and confused. She knew something was wrong, but she wasn't in a strong enough state to face what she had done to herself.

She was in a place where, unlike the higher realms, time and space still existed, and Albert said that her suicide had put her there for what would have been the remainder of her life—twenty-four years. This was what had originally propelled Chris to search for her: He couldn't bear the thought of his soul mate existing in a self-created Hell for more than two decades of her time. He was even more horrified when he actually saw the squalor of her dwelling place.

Ann showed no recognition when Chris found her. Whenever he asked her questions designed to jog her memory, Ann's eyes glazed over, and she lapsed into a state of self-isolation and inner reflection that was completely colored by despair. When Chris stopped talking, Ann meandered around the house as if he wasn't there. She preoccupied herself with petty details of the dilapidated house.

It was love, however, that finally awakened Ann, though it nearly cost Chris his life in the higher realms. After exhausting his every idea for awakening Ann to her true state, he made the decision stay there with her and make her Hell their Heaven. He would remain there with

Ann, if he couldn't bring her out—the ultimate sacrifice. He thanked her for all the wonderful things they had shared in their lives together. As he was slipping into the same state of mind as Ann, forgetting about his former life in Summerland, forgetting himself, Ann finally roused to a full awakening and recognized who Chris was.

"Is it really you?" she murmured.
"Yes, Ann. Really," Chris said.
"You did this . . . for me?" Ann asked.
"Yes, Ann. Yes."

Ann was horrified as the full impact of Chris' sacrifice entered her rapidly clearing mind, and she realized that he no longer could bring himself to leave her there.

"Heaven would never be heaven without you," Chris said. "Let this hell be our heaven." Then he slipped into sleep.

Chris slept for a long time after, but when he awoke, he wasn't in the dingy confines of Ann's Hell. Instead, he was resting on a comfortable couch in the Hall of Rest, the place where many souls awaken after a long illness on earth. Chris's love for his wife had helped bring her from her self-created Hell and had given her a new opportunity at a higher spiritual life. But it also was decided that she needed to be reborn in another country and that she would have the challenge of an illness that caused severe sleep deprivation, a consequence of her having committed suicide. She had already departed for her next life on earth when Chris awakened. Because she was his soul mate, however, he was told that he would follow her in due time and their lives would reconnect, as all soul mates do, at some predestined time on earth.

Matheson wrote:

Death is not the king of terrors. Death is a friend. Consider it this way. Do you fear to sleep at night? Of course not. Because you know that you will wake again. Think of death the same way. As a sleep from which, inevitably, you will awaken. True life is a process of becoming. Death is a stage of this progression. Life is not followed by un-life. There is only a single continuity of being. We are part of a plan, never doubt that. A plan to bring each one of us to the highest level of which we are capable. The way will be dark at times but it leads, assuredly, to light . . . Never forget, however, that we pay for every act and thought and feeling we commit. One statement from the Bible says it all. Whatsoever a man soweth, that shall he also reap. People are not punished for their deeds but by them. If only everyone believed that . . . the world could change overnight.[10]

In a universe of worlds, the possibilities for our real lives—after death—are endless. We need only awaken to the reality of our true nature—as spiritual beings living for a time in one material realm of the universe—to develop to our highest potential in the highest realms. What standing can fear have in that place that is our true home?

Endnotes

Introduction
[1]Livingston, Michele, A. *Visions from Mary.* Virginia: Blue Mantle Press, 1999.

[2]Scott, Cyril, ed. *The Boy Who Saw True.* Essex, England: C.W. Daniel, Ltd., 1953. p. 242.

Chapter 1
[1]Pseudonym.

[2]*On the Death of My Son,* p. 21–22.

[3]Ibid., p. 22.

[4]Ibid., p. 25.

Chapter 2
[1]Edgar Cayce's psychic readings were organized by a numbering system to protect the recipients' identities. The first numeral identifies the recipient; the second numeral identifies the number of that reading in all the readings given for that person.

Chapter 3
[1]R.A. Moody, M.D., "On the Near–Death Experience," lecture, Virginia Beach, Va., 1996.

[2]Ibid.

[3]Ibid.

[4]Raymond A. Moody, Jr., M.D., with Paul Perry, *The Light Beyond,* NY: Bantam Books, 1988, p. 33.

[5]Kenneth Ring, *Heading Towards Omega: In Search of the Meaning of the Near-Death Experience,* NY: Quill, 1985, p. 69.

[6]George G. Ritchie, Jr., M.D., private interview with the author.

[7]R.A. Moody, *Reflections on Life After Life,* GA: Mockingbird Books, 1977, p. 26.

[8]Ibid, p. 27.

[9]H. Storm, *My Descent into Death—And the Message of Love Which Brought me Back,* MA: Clairview Books, Anthroposophic Press, 2000, p. 11.

[10]Ibid., p. 12.

[11]Ibid., p. 20, 21.

[12]Ibid., p. 31, 32.

[13]Ibid., p. 35.

[14]H.L. Cayce, *Dimensions of Dying and Rebirth,* VA: ARE Press, 1977, p. 68.

Chapter 4
[1]White, Stuart Edward. *The Betty Book—Excursions into the World of Other-Conscious-*

ness. New York: E.P. Dutton & Company, Inc., pp. 18.

[2]Ibid., p. 20.

[3]Ibid., p. 25.

[4]White, Stuart Edward. *The Stars are Still There*, NY: E.P. Dutton & Company, Inc., 1946.

[5]White, Stuart Edward White, Harwood. *Across the Unknown*, NY: E.P. Dutton & Company, Inc., 1939.

[6]White, Stuart Edward, *The Betty Book*, p. 94.

[7]Ibid., p. 42.

[8]Ibid., p. 108.

[9]Ibid., p. 115.

[10]Greaves, Helen, *Testimony of Light*, Essex: England, C.W. Daniel Company, Ltd., 1969.

[11]*Testimony of Light*, p. 124–125.

[12]*The Betty Book*, p. 102–104.

[13]Ibid., p. 143.

[14]Cayce, Hugh Lynn. "The First Ten Minutes After Death," lecture, Virginia Beach, Va., 1976.

[15]White, Stuart Edward, *The Betty Book*, p. 149.

[16]Ibid., p. 147.

[17]Ibid., p. 159, 160.

[18]White, Stuart Edward, *Across the Unknown*, p. 332.

[19]White, Stuart Edward, *The Stars are Still There*, p. 16.

[20]White, Stuart Edward, *The Unobstructed Universe*, p. 18–19.

[21]Ibid., p. 26.

[22]White, Stuart Edward, *The Unobstructed Universe*, p. 33–34.

[23]Ibid., p. 34–35.

[24]Ibid., p. 35.

[25]Ibid., p. 36, 37.

[26]White, Stuart Edward. *The Stars are Still There*, p. 22.

[27]Ibid., p. 23.

[28]Ibid., p. 24–25.

[29]Conducted by the author during public lecture forums, 2000–2002.

[30]White, Stuart Edward, *The Stars are Still There*, p. 25–26.

[31]Ibid., p. 32.

[32]White, Stuart Edward, *The Unobstructed Universe*, p. 211–212.

Chapter 5

[1]Private interview with Hugh Lynn Cayce, 1981.

[2]Cayce, Edgar, *What I Believe*, VA: Virginia Beach, 1946, p 22–24.

[3]Leadbeater, C.W. *The Inner Life Volume I*. Illinois: The Theosophical Press, 1942.

[4]Ibid., p. 5–6.

[5]Ibid., p. 14.

[6]Scott, Cyril, ed. *The Boy Who Saw True*. Essex, England: The C.W. Daniel Co., Ltd., 1953.

[7]Ibid., p. 78–79.

[8]Ibid., p. 80.

[9]Ibid., p. 65.

[10]Ibid., p. 196.

[11]Ibid., p. 197–198.

[12]Ibid., p. 199.

[13]Ibid., p. 199–200.

Chapter 6

[1]Flower Newhouse was a renowned visionary who wrote many books, including Natives of Eternity. Edgar Cayce said in a reading that she was the best authority to provide information describing the different branches of the angelic hierarchies.

[2]Newhouse, Flower A. *The Christward Way*. California: Christward Publications, 1948, p. 38.

[3]Scott, Cyril, ed. *The Boy Who Saw True*, p. 124.

[4]Newhouse, Flower A. *Here Are Your Answers*. California: Christward Publications, 1948, p. 22–23.

[5]Bach, Richard. *Illusions—The Adventures of a Reluctant Messiah*. New York: Delacorte Press, 1977, p. 132

[6]Cayce, H.L., *Dimensions of Dying and Rebirth*. Virginia: A.R.E. Press, 1977, p. 40, 41.

[7]Moody, R., *Reflections on Life After Life*, Georgia: Mockingbird Books, 1977, p. 41–42.

[8]Ritchie, George G., M.D. Michigan: Baker Book House Company, 1978.

[9]Scott, C., ed., *The Boy Who Saw True*, p. 142–143, 145.

[10]Ibid., p. 146

Chapter 7

[1]Matheson, Richard. *What Dreams May Come*. New York: Tor Books, 1998.

[2]Ibid, p. i.

[3]Ibid, p. 60.

[4]Ibid, p. 92.

[5]Ibid, p. 90–91.

[6]ibid, p. 122.

[7]Ibid, p. 146–147.

[8]Borgia, Anthony. *Life in the Unseen World.* London: Oldhams Press, Ltd., 1954, p. 137–138.

[9]Matheson, R. *What Dreams May Come*, p. 189.

[10]Ibid, p. 265.

Bibliography and Suggested Reading List

Besant, Annie, and Leadbeater, C.W. *Thought-Forms* (abridged). Illinois: The Theosophical Publishing House, 1969.

Borgia, Anthony. *Life in the Unseen World*. London: Odhams Press, Ltd., 1954.

Cayce, Edgar. *Auras: An Essay on the Meaning of Colors*. Virginia: A.R.E. Press, 1945.

————. *What I Believe*. Virginia: A.R.E. Press, 1946.

Cayce, Hugh Lynn. *The Dimensions of Dying and Rebirth*. Virginia: A.R.E. Press, 1977.

Callanan, Maggie, and Kelley, Patricia. *Final Gifts—Understanding the Special Awareness, Needs, and Communications of the Dying*. New York: Bantam Books, 1992.

Conan Doyle, Arthur. *The New Revelation*. New York: George H. Doran, 1918.

de Hoven, Anna. *A Cloud of Witnesses*. New York: E.P. Dutton & Co., 1920.

Desmond, Shaw. *You Can Speak With Your Dead*. London: Methuen & Co., 1941.

Dresser, C. *Spirit World and Spirit Life*. San Jose, Calif.: Cosmos Publishing Co., 1927.

Ebon, Martin. *They Knew the Unknown*. New York: The World Publishing Co., 1971.

Ford, Arthur. *The Life Beyond Death*. New York: Berkley Medallion Books, 1971.

Grant, Robert J. *The Place We Call Home—Exploring the Soul's Existence after Death*. Virginia: A.R.E. Press, 2000.

Hampton, Charles. *The Transition Called Death*. Illinois: Theosophical Publishing
House, 1943.

Heindel, Max. *The Passing—and Life Afterward*. Oceanside, Calif: Rosicrucian Fel-
lowship, 1971.

Hatfield, Wayne. *Letters from Janice—Correspondence from the Astral Plane*. Missouri:
Uni? Sun Books, 1987.

Ireland–Frey, Louise, M.D. O *Sane and Sacred Death*. California: Blue Dolphin Publishing, Inc., 2002.

Gurney, Edmund, Myers, F.W.H., Podmore, Frank. *Phantasms of the Living*. New
York: E.P. Dutton and Co., 1918.

Knight, David C., ed. *The ESP Reader*. New York: Grosset & Dunlap, Inc., 1969.

Kübler–Ross, Elisabeth, M.D. *The Wheel of Life—A Memoir of Living and Dying*. New
York: Scribner, 1997.

Leadbeater C.W. *The Inner Life*. Illinois: The Theosophical Press, 1942.

Lodge, Sir Oliver J. Raymond. New York: George H. Doran Company, 1916.

Moody, Raymond A., Jr. *Life After Life—The Investigation of a Phenomenon—Survival of
Bodily Death*. New York: Bantam Books, 1975.

Morse, Melvin, M.D., Perry, Paul. *Closer to the Light—Learning from the Near-Death
Experiences of Children*. New York: Ivy Books, 1990.

Matheson, Richard. *What Dreams May Come*. New York: Tor Books, 1978.

Newton, Michael, Ph.D. *Destiny of Souls: New Case Studies of Life Between Lives.* Minnesota: Llewellyn Publications, 2002.

Patterson, Doris T. *The Unfettered Mind—Varieties of ESP in the Edgar Cayce Readings.* Virginia: A.R.E. Press, 1968.

Rinpoche, Sogyal. *The Tibetan Book of Living and Dying.* New York: Harper San Francisco, 1992.

Rogo, D. Scott. *The Infinite Boundary—A Psychic Look at Spirit Possession, Madness, and Multiple Personality.* New York: Dodd, Mead & Company, 1987.

Scott, Cyril, ed. *The Boy Who Saw True.* Essex, England: C.W. Daniel Company, Ltd., 1953.

Smith, Susy. *The Book of James.* New York: G.P. Putnam's Sons, 1974.

Snead, W.T. *After Death—New and Enlarged Edition of Letters from Julia.* New York: George H. Doran Co., 1914.

Storm, Howard. *My Descent into Death.* Massachusetts: Clairview Books, 2000.

Sutherland, Cherie, Ph.D. *Reborn in the Light—Life After Near-Death Experiences.* New York: Bantam Books, 1992.

Swain, Jasper. *On the Death of My Son—An Account of Life After Death.* Northamptonshire, England: Aquarian Press, 1989.

White, Edward Stuart. *The Betty Book—Excursions into the World of Other-Consciousness.* NY: E.P. Dutton & Company, Inc., 1946.

—*Across the Unknown.* NY: E.P. Dutton & Company, Inc., 1946.

—*The Unobstructed Universe.* NY: E.P. Dutton & Company, Inc., 1940.

—*The Road I Know.* NY: E.P. Dutton & Company, Inc., 1946.

—*The Stars Are Still There.* NY: E.P. Dutton & Company, Inc., 1946.

A.R.E. PRESS

The A.R.E. Press publishes books, videos, and audiotapes meant to improve the quality of our readers' lives—personally, professionally, and spiritually. We hope our products support your endeavors to realize your career potential, to enhance your relationships, to improve your health, and to encourage you to make the changes necessary to live a loving, joyful, and fulfilling life.

For more information or to receive a free catalog, call:

1–800–723–1112

Or write:

A.R.E. Press
215 67th Street
Virginia Beach, VA 23451–2061